Socialisation During the Life Course

This comprehensive text highlights new developments in sociological, educational and psychological aspects of socialisation, examining how human beings as 'subjects' – experiencing, thinking and acting individuals – confront the material, social and cultural 'objects' of their environment and sustain their position. The authors provide an overview of the most important theories of socialisation, then integrate these using the Productive Processing of Reality (PPR) model. This novel approach is applied to a life course analysis, examining developmental tasks and the challenges of productive processing of the internal and external reality at various stages of development. The book also considers contexts, addressing the inequalities between different socio-economic and ethnic groups and genders, to consider how humans – with their genetic dispositions and their individual instincts and needs – solve the task of coping with the requirements of society, culture and economy while at the same time safeguarding their status as unique individuals.

It is core reading for advanced students on socialisation modules in developmental or social psychology and educational sciences and is additionally of value for the professional training of sociologists, teachers and social workers. It is also relevant for all those interested in elementary questions of how the interaction between the society and the individual works; how human beings deal not only with themselves, but also with their social and physical environment, and how they shape it in their own way.

Klaus Hurrelmann is Senior Professor of Public Health and Education at Hertie School of Governance in Berlin. He previously served as Professor of Socialisation at Bielefeld University in Germany.

Ullrich Bauer is Professor of Socialisation Research at the Faculty of Educational Science and Head of the Center for Prevention in Childhood and Adolescence at Bielefeld University in Germany.

Socialisation During the Life Course

Klaus Hurrelmann
and Ullrich Bauer

Routledge
Taylor & Francis Group

LONDON AND NEW YORK

First published 2018
by Routledge
2 Park Square, Milton Park, Abingdon, Oxon OX14 4RN

and by Routledge
711 Third Avenue, New York, NY 10017

Routledge is an imprint of the Taylor & Francis Group, an informa business

British Library Cataloguing-in-Publication Data
A catalogue record for this book is available from the British Library

Library of Congress Cataloging-in-Publication Data
Hurrelmann, Klaus, author. | Bauer, Ullrich, author.
Socialisation during the life course/Klaus Hurrelmann and Ullrich Bauer.
Other titles: Socialization during the life course
Description: New York: Routledge, 2018. | Includes bibliographical
references and index.
Identifiers: LCCN 2017034755| ISBN 9781138502178 (hb: alk. paper) |
ISBN 9781138502185 (pb: alk. paper) | ISBN 9781315144801 (eb)
Subjects: LCSH: Socialisation. | Life cycle, Human.
Classification: LCC HM686 .H87 2018 | DDC 303.3/2–dc23
LC record available at https://lccn.loc.gov/2017034755

ISBN: 978-1-138-50217-8 (hbk)
ISBN: 978-1-138-50218-5 (pbk)
ISBN: 978-1-315-14480-1 (ebk)

Typeset in Optima
by Florence Production Ltd, Stoodleigh, Devon, UK

The authors would like to thank Angelika Behlen and Dayna Sadow for their insightful work on the manuscript.

Contents

About the authors

Klaus Hurrelmann is Senior Professor of Public Health and Education at Hertie School of Governance in Berlin, Germany. He studied sociology, psychology and education in Berkeley (USA), Freiburg and Muenster (Germany). In 1975, he took on a professorship for empirical social research at the University of Essen. In 1980, he transferred to Bielefeld University as Professor of Socialisation. With his colleagues, he established the Interdisciplinary Research Centre Prevention and Inter-vention in Childhood and Youth (SFB 227, financed by the German Research Association) and served as its director from 1986 to 1998. He was also co-founder of the Centre for Childhood and Youth Research in Bielefeld. In 1994, he joined the newly established Faculty of Health Sciences at Bielefeld University and held the office of Founding Dean for almost 10 years. He worked in the area of prevention and health promotion and initiated international research projects. On behalf of the World Health Organization (WHO), he served as the Director of the Collaborating Research Centre for Health in Adolescence until 2007 and headed the German section of the research project Health Behaviour in School Children (HBSC). He was a Visiting Professor of Sociology of Education at New York University in 1990 and of Public Health and Education at UCLA in 1999. In 2009, Klaus Hurrelmann joined the Hertie

School of Governance in Berlin as Senior Professor of Public Health and Education.

Ullrich Bauer is Professor of Socialisation Research at Bielefeld University in Germany. He heads the Centre for Prevention and Intervention in Childhood and Adolescence (CPI) at the Faculty of Educational Science. He is trained in Sociology and Public Health. He formerly held positions with the Faculty of Educational Sciences, University of Duisburg-Essen, the School of Public Health, Bielefeld University and the Social Research Centre WZB in Berlin. Ullrich Bauer pursues research questions in health-related socialisation and education research. This focus includes especially the topic of socialisation processes with a special consideration of vulnerable groups with limited resources. He is heading research projects in the area of stress experience and stress consequences in children (6–12-years-of-age) of mentally ill parents (EEEIPP project), on the educational careers of adolescents from socially disadvantaged groups (HABIL project), and on developing and evaluating health promotion programmes. He also heads the German consortium 'Health Literacy in Childhood and Adolescence' HLCA. He has expertise in health-related socialisation and educational processes with a particular focus on vulnerable groups with limited resources. He currently runs two national research consortiums.

The understanding of socialisation

The concept of socialisation is used in many academic disciplines to describe the personality development of human beings in permanent interaction with their physical and psychological disposition on the one hand and the social and ecological living conditions on the other. The term first appeared in sociology and psychology, was then adopted by educational science, and later on by social work and social pedagogy. During the past 20 years, it has also become popular in health sciences and public health, in some areas of paediatrics, adolescent and social medicine, as well as in nursing science and related disciplines.

In this book, we apply this approach to the analysis of the human life course in modern societies. As socialisation is characterised by the permanent confrontation with internal and external requirements, this life-course perspective is self-evident. The fundamental question is how it is possible for human beings to plan their lives consistently during times of economic turbulence and political crises. Consequently, this approach implies a meta-theoretical perspective. This means, first, that we tend to provide a bird's eye perspective rather than a compartmentalised argumentation of different theoretical features of socialisation research. Although socialisation is seen as a sociological key concept tackling basic problems of ensuring social order (Bühler-Niederberger, 2016) the general framework refers to a more individual perspective of dispositions, competencies and personality development (Grusec and Hastings, 2016). This implies, second, a constant mediating process between structure and agency (Archer, 2012). And, third, although most approaches highlight a childhood perspective (Denzin, 2010; Mcnamee, 2016; Qvortrup, Corsaro and Honig, 2009) a broader socialisation perspective only starts with a focus on childhood (Lancy, Bock and Gaskins, 2010) and widens towards a life-course perspective that encompasses lifelong person-environment-interactions from an individual's perspective. This is what we will call *'productive processing of reality'* in the following argumentation. It serves as an overarching hook of theorising socialisation during the life course.

In this chapter, we start with a discussion of everyday and the scientific understanding of socialisation. In Chapter 2, we turn to our own approach of a comprehensive theory of socialisation according to the 'Model of Productive Processing of Reality (PPR)', which integrates different individual theories. This approach is then transferred to life-course analysis. In a first step, we analyse the developmental tasks to be solved in different life stages (Chapter 3). In a second step, we discuss the productive processing of the internal and external reality during the life course in general (Chapter 4) and during the four stages childhood, adolescence, adulthood and old age in specific (Chapter 5). Thereafter we discuss the framework conditions and contexts needed by human beings to manage a productive processing of internal and external reality (Chapter 6) and address the enormous inequality between different groups of society – according to socioeconomic status, gender and ethnic background – which results from the qualitative differences in productive processing (Chapter 7). The book ends with an outlook on future challenges of socialisation research in Chapter 8.

Everyday understanding of socialisation

The term socialisation is one of the scholarly terms that are not only used in a great variety of academic disciplines but also in everyday life. Expressions such as *'This child is well socialised'* or *'This shows your socialisation as a diplomat'* point to the substance of this term: the integration of social values and norms, the adaptation to the social environment, the endeavour to *become-what-society-expects-me-to-be,* or even the concept of the conditioning of individuals by the social context, that is the process of becoming social. However, everyday language also knows that a child can *'leave socialisation behind'* and a diplomat can *'step out of the shadows of socialisation'*, expressing that the development of an independent personality is possible and that an individual evades environmental influences to a certain extent and even actively influences the development of his or her environment.

Socialisation as reciprocal person–environment relationship

This double perspective is fully adopted in everyday understanding. It is consistent with the experiences made by human beings. Each person intuitively knows the 'effects' of a specific external influence, such as unemployment due to economic trends following the global economic crisis from 2007 to 2008, for example. This is dependent not only upon the intensity and duration but also upon the personal characteristics and initial condition of the individual affected by such influences. Many people feel helpless and depressed when affected by unemployment; others react with resistance and activate their survival skills.

The influence of environmental events is by no means a one-way street. Even if the influences of the social environment, of the respective social, economical and cultural setting in which a person lives, are important, have enduring effects and leave lasting marks on his or her attitude and action patterns – this alone is not sufficient to determine the personality development of this person to the full extent. Therefore, *homogamy*, the equivalence of biographically experienced and current action structures is by no means the rule. Rather, the social environments encountered during the life course are subject to permanent historical change. New influences appear, and others disappear. Thus, the action competences once acquired are by no means applicable to all subsequent situations and great efforts are constantly required to adapt to new or altered challenges.

Determinants of socialisation

This is also true at the level of direct personal contacts. The relations between a person and his or her environment are reciprocal and interactive. The question of how a specific external influence 'takes effect' can only be answered with a view to the initial conditions of this individual.

Here is an everyday life example:

> *At 10.30 p.m., a 17-year-old adolescent waits for his connecting train at the underground station in the centre of a large city. Someone taps him on the shoulder from behind. How does he react? His reaction will depend on his biographical experience and his perception of the situation. Situational: He can be in a bad mood (after a long workday and a failed exam in the morning) or in a good mood (after a shopping trip with friends) and*

therefore be open or not open for the question signalised by the tap on the shoulder. Biographical: He may come from an environment in which he experiences a great amount of aggression, disposing him to react immediately to a movement from behind which is directly addressing his body, and whip round prepared to defend himself, or attack. But he might also have bad experiences with such a reaction and decide to refrain from using force. Maybe he expects an aggressive action in return and took the decision to resist this dynamic. We can also imagine the 17-year-old young man as a violinist who is just returning from a rehearsal with his ensemble and has no manifest idea of violence or counter violence and reacts completely defensive; or a religious person who rejects violence completely due to his intensive religious conviction.

With the situational and biographical background information of this example, we have narrowed down two of the influences belonging to the conditions, which determine the possible reactions of a person in a specific situation. Gender and religion are other factors that point to common attitudes in different ways. The example shows that the reaction of the 17-year-old person to the tap from behind depends on these factors. They are decisive for the following action and can be more or less conscious or reflected and thus part of reaction patterns that are a result of socialisation.

Another important aspect decisive for the reaction of the 17-year-old adolescent refers to the socio-spatial conditions. In our subway example, these are connected with contextual and compositional influences. Contextual factors concern the features of a place, for example the location of the station in the city district, and the amount of people present in the situation. Compositional factors describe the composition of the people waiting in the underground station together with the 17-year-old. The adolescent's reaction will decisively be determined by the conditions, that is whether he waits for the underground together with a group of close friends who could back him up in case of a conflict, or whether he is alone and the person tapping on his shoulder belongs to a large group of unknown young people; or whether the finger tapping on his shoulder is by an elderly lady who got lost, has been wandering around for hours and does not know how to find her way home.

The example shows that biographical, group-related and socio-spatial factors come together in a situation that only lasts for a few seconds. It is an interaction of the individual's personal determinants with those of the space or location and those of the person tapping on his shoulder. The 17-year-old adolescent assimilates the reality within seconds, processes it and reacts.

But the same is true for the person tapping on his shoulder. Both interact with each other and answer to the reactions of the other. Both call up a stock of knowledge and actions they are familiar with from their previous life experiences. Maybe the 17-year-old makes an angry face and talks loudly when he is confronted with an aggressive unknown person but puts on a friendly smile and reacts in a caring way when he sees the elderly lady.

All this is part of socialisation. It does not only take place in the individual and not only depends upon the conditions in which we act or by which we have been shaped. Our know-how is updated in the interaction, we draw on the language and experiences in dealing with elderly persons and the care they deserve, and we thereby confirm the applicability of specific behavioural patterns (Duranti, Ochs and Schieffelin, 2014). At the same time, we learn lessons from every new situation and prepare ourselves to react more favourably should we be faced with a similar situation.

Of course we are not fully aware of all these aspects when we speak about socialisation in everyday life, but the fundamental experience of the reciprocal person-environment relation exists. We are aware of the fact that every day we act in situations in which we use our knowledge and experiences to understand the circumstances and that our personal know-how and action repertoires are at the same time confirmed, revised or expanded. We also know that our personality develops constantly and on the one hand, is influenced by the material and social structures surrounding us but on the other hand also influences them.

The scientific understanding of socialisation

At the core of socialisation theory is the question of how a human being with his or her genetic disposition of instinctual drives and needs, with his or her innate temperament and acquired personality traits, as well as in interaction with the surrounding environmental factors, becomes a subject with the ability of self-reflection and manages to cope with the requirement of integration into a social fabric. To answer this question, psychological as well as sociological approaches are required.

Psychological approaches primarily address the individual's 'internal reality'. They analyse in which stages and phases human personality development takes place, how the capacities of perception, thinking and acting evolve and how they change in the phases of transition from one stage of life to the next as well as in situations of crisis and tension. During the past years, they have been increasingly supplemented by neurobiological approaches.

Sociological approaches, however, focus on 'external reality'. They analyse the structures of the human personality, which occur in confrontation with the requirements of society, such as the ability to adopt the prevailing values, norms and patterns of behaviour and to join social groups and organisations.

Early approaches

The question of how the personality of a human being develops and how this process is influenced by the environment is as old as the entire history of human and social sciences. Socialisation theory focuses on the tension between the individual and society. Two related questions are at issue here:

- How does a society manage to shape the human beings living in this society into social beings who integrate themselves in the social structures?

- How do human beings manage to open up opportunities for their own personal development and lifestyle and become autonomous individuals in a society?

Thus, it is about understanding how human beings as 'subjects' – as experiencing, thinking and acting individuals – confront the material, social and cultural 'objects' of their environment and assert themselves, how they solve the task of coping with the requirements of society, culture and economy with their specific genetic dispositions, their instincts and needs, their inherent temperament and personality traits, and at the same time safeguard their status as unique individuals.

Sociological theories of socialisation

The earliest socialisation theorists were two sociologists. The German social philosopher Georg Simmel and the French sociologist Emile Durkheim are regarded as the scientific founders of the concept of 'socialisation'. At the beginning of the twentieth century, both were mainly concerned with the question of how social cohesion could be ensured in times of fast and intensive industrialisation, which was leading to increasingly complex societies.

To answer this question, Georg Simmel took account of the phenomenon of the formation of societies. According to his explanation, societies can emerge because human beings constantly influence each other. As a result, a network of rules and dependencies is created which forms the society. In this sense, each member of the society is a 'socialised individual'. Simmel refers to this process as 'socialisation' (Simmel, 1890). By this, he essentially means the process of incorporating the social entirety into the individual personality. According to his assessment, every society needs a homogenous social awareness of its members, even if they belong to different social classes and are highly different individuals, because otherwise the society as a community will collapse.

In his analysis of the transition from simple societies to societies based on the division of labour, Emile Durkheim raised the question of how integration can be achieved in complex social structures. His answer: The society shapes the personality of human beings according to its needs by systematically influencing their feelings and attitudes. He called this influence 'socialisation méthodique' meaning the systematic and planned manipulation of the attitudes of all members of the society, with the objective to shape them according to the specific needs of the society and its economy. Most of the society members adapt to social constraints without resistance and internalise social requirements because in doing so, they profit from the advantages of community life.

For Durkheim, this 'internalisation of the social facts' is the decisive condition for the cohesion and functioning of complex societies (Durkheim, 1956/1902). The only way to ensure the survival of industrial societies is if the society permeates the individual, in a sense, and organises his or her personality from the inside. According to Durkheim, social norms encounter an individual who acts libidinously, selfishly and anti-socially and only becomes socially acceptable by the process of socialisation. In a similar sense, Simmel understood socialisation as the 'socialisation of the human nature'.

With their theoretical approaches, Simmel and Durkheim established socialisation theory by contributing systematic analytical reflections on the subject of the tension-filled interaction between the individual and society to scientific discourse. However, their ground-breaking work was only recognised and continued some decades later. In today's sociology, system theories, action theories and social theories prove to be significant for analysing the processes of the interaction of human beings with their internal and external reality.

Psychological theories of personality development

Some time later, the psychologist Sigmund Freud worked on a theory of human needs and drives, and the psychologist John B. Watson was busy on a theory of human learning. Neither used the term 'socialisation', but their interests were clearly aimed at tracing the human personality back to the intensive interaction of individuals with their social environment. In this sense, they were the first socialisation theorists in psychology.

In his psychoanalytic theory of personality, Sigmund Freud intensely discusses the biological drives and psychological needs of the human subject, but also relates them to the social constraints that humans are confronted with. According to this theory, a person's attitudes, motivations, feelings and behaviours can be traced to biological needs and drives. Parents, and particularly the mother, have the task of taming and channelling this biological disposition in order to shape the new-born 'bundle of drives' with its animalistic traits into a member of the family and society, a socially integrated being, at the very beginning of its life. With this, psychoanalytical theory refers to Durkheim's question of how the socialisation of human nature is brought about. In contrast to Durkheim, however, the answer is not sought in 'systematic education' but in the close and emotional interaction between mother, father and child (Freud, 1923/1927).

Watson's learning theory is driven by the idea that the behaviour of a human being and thus also the personality development, is influenced by impulses from the social environment. As such, the personality is not controlled by genetic factors or drives according to this theory but by the processing of influences and stimulations from the environment. Thus, a person is born without innate patterns for processing the external reality and must build up his or her behaviour on the basis of experiences. Action competences are only developed on the basis of personal interactions with the environment, which constitute learning processes. Therefore, the behaviour of a person is seen as a reaction to impulses from the environment (Watson, 1980). This demonstrates Durkheim's core idea that in the end, a human being with his or her characteristics and traits reflects the social reality and is a product of his or her environment. However, human beings are able to learn and therefore able to assimilate the stimuli and impulses from the environment in a flexible manner and process them productively to his or her advantage. With this orientation, learning theory places greater emphasis on the interaction between the individual and society and the plasticity of the human personality than the psychoanalytic theory of Freud.

Learning theories and personality theories have defined the most important trends in psychological socialisation theories up to today. In addition to this, development theories have evolved based on the psychoanalytic theory, which emphasise the emergence in phases of ever new characteristics and structures of the human personality during the life course. Following the tradition of learning theory, modern approaches of coping and mastering of stress are relevant for the understanding of socialisation

Neuro-biological theories of the dichotomy of disposition and environment

During the past three decades, neuro-biological approaches have been developed. They are rooted in neurobiology and physiology, as well as in brain research more specifically, as well as in development and evolutionary biology and neuro-pharmacology. With their focus on the interactions between the activities of the brain, the related behaviour of the individual person and environmental factors, they supplement the psychological and sociological theories described above (Anderson and Beauchamp, 2012).

Neurobiological approaches deliver interesting results on the interaction between disposition and environment. They show how close genetic dispositions and social environmental factors work together and influence each other. Hardly any of the neuroscience approaches questions the socially determined influence and impact on the human personality structure.

According to previous research, genes have no direct influence on a human being's personality and behaviour in most cases but constitute a reservoir of development opportunities from which individual elements can be activated by external impulses. Genetic impacts always develop in interaction with the environment of the genome. Even the development of the intelligence quotient (IQ) is not only genetically determined but mainly a result of the interaction between disposition and environmental stimuli (Blakemore, 2008; Bruer, 1999).

The human brain is apparently created in such a way that it does not just constitute a passive point of reception for sensory input and reality information but constantly performs comparisons and classifications, offers combinations and conclusions and not only provides humans with the ability to act and react but also constantly challenges this ability. The brain is in a way the coordination and control centre for the 'productive processing of reality'.

All in all, the findings of neurobiology, and particularly those of epigenetics, can be interpreted to the effect that the dichotomy of disposition and environment is suspended, because the genetic disposition cannot be considered as a mechanical determinant of the human development but always operates in a 'dialogue' with the environment. Thus, the environment influences even the genetic structure. If the genetic or epigenetic structure takes effect, then in a variant in which the person-environment interaction already took place. The neurobiological approaches that virtually permeate the core of the human personality show very clearly that a person does not develop gradually 'programmed' by his or her disposition but that a lifelong interplay between the internal reality of genetic disposition and the external reality of environmental factors takes place.

Questions

1   What is the definition of socialisation?

2   What are the two core questions focusing on the tension between the individual and the society?

3   What answer did the founding fathers of sociological socialisation theory, Georg Simmel and Emile Durkheim, give to these questions?

4   What answer did the founding fathers of psychological socialisation theory, Sigmund Freud and John B. Watson, give to these questions?

5   What are the core assumptions of neuro-biological theories of socialisation?

Answers .

1   Socialisation is a technical term used in many academic disciplines to describe the personality development of human beings in permanent interaction with their physical and psychological disposition on the one hand and the social and ecological living conditions on the other.

2   (A) How does a society manage to shape the human beings living in this society into social beings who integrate themselves in the social structures? (B) How do human beings manage to open up opportunities for their own personal development and lifestyle and become autonomous individuals in a society?

3   According to Durkheim, social norms encounter an individual who acts libidinously, selfishly and anti-socially and only becomes socially acceptable by the process of socialisation. Most of the society members adapt to social constraints without resistance and internalise social requirements because in doing so, they profit from the advantages of community life. In a similar vein Simmel proclaims that every society needs a homogenous social awareness of its members, even if they belong to different social classes, because otherwise the society as a community will collapse.

4   In his psychoanalytic theory of personality, Sigmund Freud intensely discusses the biological drives and psychological needs of the human subject, but also relates them to the social contexts and constraints that humans are confronted with. According to Watson the behaviour of a human being, and thus also the personality development, is influenced by impulses from the social environment. As such, the

personality essentially is not controlled by genetic factors or drives but by the processing of influences and stimulations from the environment.

5   Neurobiological approaches deliver results on the interaction between disposition and environment. They show how close genetic dispositions and social environmental factors work together and influence each other. Genes have no direct influence on a human being's personality and behaviour in most cases but constitute a reservoir of development opportunities from which individual elements can be activated by external impulses.

Socialisation as productive processing of reality

The description of the various theoretical approaches shows that each of the theories mentioned makes a contribution to understanding the interaction between the individual and society, but each theory does this in its own way and with its own terminology and methodology. None of the theories can claim to cover the entire scope of 'socialisation', for each of them approaches the topic from a specific perspective that sheds light on some elements of the subject matter but leaves others in the dark.

It is therefore useful to combine suitable theories with their respective achievements and perspectives. If they are well geared to each other, socialisation can be analysed from several perspectives and perceived in its entirety. This is successful especially if theoretical approaches of the sociological as well as the psychological and the neurobiological traditions are combined, as they start out from different perspectives.

The combination of sociological, psychological and neurobiological theories

The concept of a 'comprehensive' socialisation theory suggested by us is based on this idea. We expect a gain of knowledge if sociological, psychological and neurobiological theories are carefully combined. This creates an analytical double perspective because theories, which are based on the explanatory variable 'society', are combined with theories, which are based on the explanatory variable 'individual'.

- The sociological theories based on Simmel and Durkheim focus on the interaction between the individual and society and the tension-filled balancing of individual needs and safeguarding identity on the one hand and social integration requirements on the other. This also applies to action theories and system theories that have grown out of the traditional approaches by Simmel and Durkheim: The approach of Mead's action theory with the concept of the human being as creative designer of his or her social environment is ground-breaking for this view (Mead, 1934), and also Parsons in his system theory with his concept of the interpenetration of the systems organism, person and society points in this direction (Parsons, 1951). Social milieu theories, and particularly that of Bourdieu (1980/1990), also follow this line. Nearly all of these theories emphasise the human subject's own efforts of personality development and individuation. They try to identify the mechanisms through which external, social influences affect internal, personal characteristics and structures. They point to the social and cultural expectations of the environment, the requirements and stimuli of concrete social and ecological living environments and the possibilities of a person to shape his or her personality through active interaction with the social environment.

- The psychological theories based on Freud and Watson work out that human personality development is strongly influenced not only by internal factors anchored within the person but also by external, social factors: Erikson's (1964/1968) personality theory, as well as the development theories of Lerner (1976) and Bronfenbrenner (1979), refer to the social and cultural expectations imposed on a human being. At the same time, they all take into account the requirements and stimuli that result from the concrete social living environments. The learning theory of Bandura (1977) and the coping theory of Antonovsky (1979) elaborate the possibilities available to a human being to influence his or her personality by way of active interaction with the social environment. Although the term 'socialisation' is used rather reluctantly in these theories because of its sociological origin, the psychological theories discuss the core issue of the relation between individual and society in great detail. They take emotional and cognitive intra-psychic structural developments as a starting point and are primarily concerned with the question of how the personality of a human being unfolds and changes during the life course through social and ecological environmental conditions. Thereby, they fundamentally complement the sociological positions.

- The recent approaches of the neurosciences mirror this knowledge and confirm the influence of variably stimulating environments. As already mentioned they show how close genetic dispositions and social environmental factors work together and influence each other. They open up the window to the internal absorption of environmental experiences and their transmission to neural connections, brain structures and epigenetic processing.

The development of the 'Model of Productive Processing of Reality' (PPR)

The idea of a comprehensive, interdisciplinary socialisation theory is based on the analytical double perspective of the explanatory variables 'society' and 'individual'. The two processes of 'becoming societal' and 'becoming individual' are seen as interdependent and balanced.

To outline a comprehensive socialisation theory, an exemplary model encompassing the individual theories is required that serves as the frame for a 'meta-theory'. The meta-theory is encompassing the individual theories mentioned above, combining them to an 'entirety' (Hurrelmann and Ulich, 1980, p. 8). In this understanding, socialisation serves as a categorical supra-concept for the organisation and integration of a number of issues to be explained respectively by specific theories.

The meta-theoretical model is named '*Productive Processing of Reality*' *(PPR)*. It places the human subject in a social and ecological context which is absorbed and processed individually, which in this sense acts on the subject but at the same time is always influenced, changed and shaped by the subject. The model incorporates the traditional concept of socialisation as the adoption of norms but refines it on the basis of the idea of individual appropriation and shaping that is derived from modern sociological, psychological and neurobiological approaches (Bauer, 2013; Hurrelmann, 1988).

The definition of socialisation

The definition of 'socialisation' that refers to this model can be phrased as follows:

> *Socialisation describes the personality development of a human being, which results from the productive processing of the internal and external reality. The physical and mental dispositions and characteristics constitute the 'internal' reality, the conditions of the social and physical environment the 'external' reality. The processing of reality is 'productive' because a person always deals with life in an active manner and tries to cope with the developmental tasks connected with it. Whether or not the individual is successful in coping with these tasks depends on the personal and social resources available to him or her. The demand to balance personal individualisation and social integration in order to safeguard the self-identity is present in all phases of life and development.*

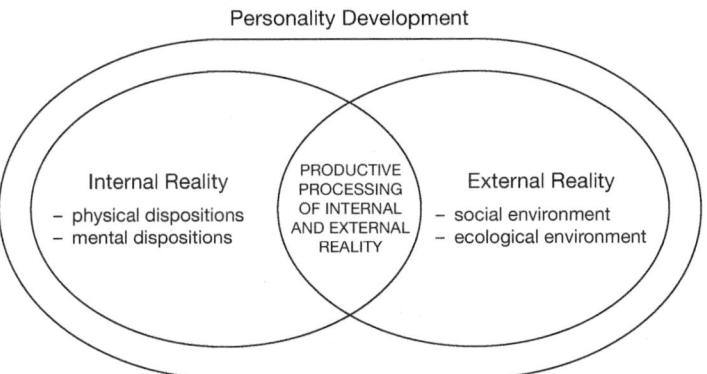

Figure 2.1 Socialisation as personality development in the format of productive processing of internal and external reality

Figure 2.1 depicts the core elements of this definition. This definition includes some assumptions that are important to understand socialisation:

- *First* it explains socialisation as a process of 'personality development': the individually specific and unique structure of physical and psychological traits, characteristics and dispositions of a human being is designated as personality. Personality 'development' can thus be understood as the change of essential elements in this structure during the course of life. As environment-related beings who are able to learn, humans change their coping strategies and construct their own personal history ('biography') in accordance with the challenges encountered during the life course, while the basic structure of their personality remains the same.

- *Second* socialisation is described as 'productive processing of reality': As a result, a lifelong active process by a human being of acquiring and processing natural dispositions and social and physical environmental conditions is postulated. Thus, the personality development of a human is neither determined by his or her dispositions nor by the environment; instead, the personality unfolds in the interplay between these variables.

- *Third* coping with developmental tasks is seen as a permanent requirement to socialisation: In every life stage, there are specific expectations which must be met for the processing of reality which stem from physical and psychological development and the social environment.

Key assumptions of the model of PPR

The socialisation theory presented by us is based on the essential assumption that the personality development of human beings takes place in the interaction between disposition and environment. The biological and genetic characteristics (or the genotype as entirety of genetic dispositions) determine general development opportunities over the entire course of life. But genes do not influence the personality and behaviour of a human being directly. Instead, they determine the space of possibilities from which individual elements can be activated. At the same time they limit the development potential of a person, as he or she is not able to go beyond the given dispositions. The extent to which the disposition as internal reality and the environment as external reality influence personality development can not be exactly determined; however, the findings of current interdisciplinary research suggest that this influence is more or less balanced (Wozniak and Fischer, 2014).

The active and constant individual effort of coping with the internal and external reality is referred to as 'processing' in this hypothesis. The term 'processing' describes not only the permanent, mainly unconscious, interaction between person and environment, but also the constant work on the own personality over the entire life course. Thus, 'processing' emphasises the permanent personal contribution of humans in the development of their characteristics and traits, as well as in the selection and determination of their social acts. A person's subjective perception includes the concept of body and psyche, as well as of the social and physical environment. Internal and external reality is always experienced through the filter of one's own subjective perception, and therefore every concept of the internal and external reality is individual.

The construct 'individual' that forms the basis of psychological theories is defined as 'internal reality', which is determined by genetic disposition, physical constitution, intelligence, psychological temperament and the fundamental structure of the personality. The construct 'society' that is the basis of sociological theories, constitutes the 'external reality' consisting of family, living conditions, friends and peer groups, educational institutions, work places, leisure and media offerings and politics, as well as of the physical environment of spaces and places, natural living conditions and nutrition offers.

The term 'productive processing' expresses that the individual effort to cope with the internal and external reality is an active process in which people choose their own way in line with their own requirements and needs. Processing is 'productive' because it results from the specific, individual way of dealing with the internal and external conditions. However, the term does not indicate whether processing is successfully managed in a way that supports further personality development, if problems or crises in the personality development are actually coped with successfully. The word 'productive' is not used as an evaluative but as a descriptive term.

The production of the own personality

Highly developed societies offer a particularly high degree of freedom to shape one's own personality, because the traditionally fixed definitions regarding social roles and cultural norms no longer prevail, which allows more leeway for most people to shape their individual profile and to actively develop the own personality. This includes the patterns of motivation and meaning, the creation of continuity in the individual biography and the cumulative principle of the coherent coordination of previous experiences and those experiences, which are directly linked to the available dispositions.

Human beings are 'producers' of their own development because they process their internal and external reality in accordance with their individual characteristics and personal resources from the early stages of development as an infant and small child, through adolescence and adulthood up until old age. In this process, their personality is formed and develops step by step on the basis of the interaction between available and acquired individual characteristics, as well as the material, social and symbolic features of their environment. In this process, the developing personality is not just passively accepting or observing but is a creative constructor actively involved in shaping the own biography.

Personality development includes the acceptance of one's own physical and psychological dispositions and their changes during the course of life. It is essential to be aware of the possibilities available through internal dispositions for the management of the own individual personality, but at the same time to also recognise all chances of development that arise from the external conditions. The greater the margin that human beings capture for the productive processing of their internal and external reality, the better the possibilities are to co-create the social and physical reality and try behavioural patterns that are particularly suited to fulfil their own needs in these newly developed fields.

Independent activity requires that a person draws on a complex reservoir of reaction and action patterns during his or her personality development that allows the use of strategies *dealing with* reality on the basis of the perception and evaluation (*processing* of reality) of the complex requirements of the environment. *Dealing with* reality means the ability to react to the requirements of the environment by acting consciously and thereby manage the personal development independently (Hurrelmann, 1988, p. 42). Thus, the individual human being is the action centre. This action centre is controlled by the *action competences* available for the concrete coordination of actions. Accordingly, action competences mean the individual state of availability and adequate application of skills and abilities for coping with the external and internal reality. They constitute the starting point for social and instrumental actions. They enable the individual to cope with medium or long-term situational requirements characterised by external expectations on the one hand and the acting person's own needs, desires and objectives on the other hand.

Questions

1   What is the idea of the meta-theoretical model named *'Model of Productive Processing of Reality'* *(PPR)*?

2   What is the definition of 'socialisation' that refers to this model?

3   What is the essential meaning of the term 'productive processing of internal and external reality'?

4   What is the definition of internal reality?

5   What is the definition of external reality?

6   In which respect can individuals be considered to be producers of their own development?

Answers

1   This model places the human subject in a social and ecological context that acts on the subject, but at the same time is always influenced, changed and shaped by the subject. This process is called 'productive processing of internal and external reality'. The physical and mental dispositions and characteristics constitute the internal reality, the conditions of the social and physical environment the external reality. The processing of reality is 'productive' because a person always deals with life in an active manner and tries to cope with the developmental tasks connected with it.

2   Socialisation describes the personality development of a human being which results from the productive processing of the internal and external reality.

3   The term describes not only the permanent, mainly unconscious, interaction between person and environment but also the constant work on the own personality over the entire life course. Processing emphasises the permanent personal contribution of humans in the development of their characteristics and traits, as well as in the selection and determination of their social acts.

4   Internal reality is determined by genetic disposition, physical constitution, intelligence, psychological temperament and the fundamental structure of the personality.

5   External reality consists of family, living conditions, friends and peer groups, educational institutions, work places, leisure and media offerings and politics, as well as of the physical environment of spaces and places, natural living conditions and nutrition offers.

6   They process their internal and external reality in accord-
    ance with their individual characteristics and personal
    resources from the early stages of development as an infant
    and small child, through adolescence and adulthood up
    until old age. In this process, their personality develops
    constantly on the basis of the interaction between avail-
    able and acquired individual characteristics, as well as the
    material, social and symbolic features of their environment.

CHAPTER

3

Coping with developmental tasks

During the course of their lives, human beings are permanently confronted with new situations, which have to be managed by using adequate forms of action. Human beings are consistently challenged – particularly during severe social or economic crises and/or in times of radical biographic changes and transitions – to activate their coping capacities. To analyse these processes, the concept of developmental tasks provides a helpful orientation pattern. It can be found in the psychological theories of Erik H. Erikson (1964, 1968) and Robert J. Havighurst (1953). On the basis of this concept, social requirements and the individual developmental processes can be compared, and specific 'milestones' identified.

Developmental tasks during the life course

A developmental task describes the profile of individual action competences in dealing with the body, psyche, and social and material environment, which is expected for a specific stage of life. Every person must manage this in his or her own individual way. Coping with these tasks requires a reconciliation of the biological and psychological requirements of internal reality with the social and ecological requirements of external reality. The biological and psychological requirements of the individual life stages are universal, and must therefore be managed in each culture according to largely predetermined patterns. The social and ecological requirements differ greatly according to the state of the political, economic and cultural development of a society.

In modern democratic European societies with a relatively high level of wealth, there are usually more margins for shaping one's own individual way of life than, for instance, in an autocratic African society with a low level of prosperity. An example for this is the possibility to decide upon the course of education, training and occupational activities that can be shaped according to personal priorities; another example is the structure of gender roles, which are not bound to fixed cultural stereotypes. In democratic societies, cultural and social standards are generally no longer as normalised as in non-democratic societies and offer individuals a greater variety of ways to cope with age-specific developmental tasks according to their own preferences.

Coping with developmental tasks

In every life stage, there are specific expectations which must be met for the processing of reality which stem from physical and psychological development and the social environment. A person must accept the largely biologically predetermined physical changes and adapt his or her behaviour accordingly. It is also expected that the changes in the psychological state are accepted and expressed in their behaviour in an adequate manner. These expectations are the basis of 'developmental tasks'. They describe the behaviour considered adequate for a child, an adolescent, an adult or a senior. They must be defined by each person, translated into the own action repertoire and managed in their own specific way.

The developmental tasks in the individual life stages can essentially be described as follows:

- Early childhood is about developing the basic sensory and motoric abilities, bonding with a primary reference person and later on establishing social contacts to peers and training language and perception. In primary school, intellectual abilities and the compliance with social norms are required.

- Adolescence is about accepting the changes in the physique, developing a gender identity, strengthening school performance, starting to detach from the parents, building up relationships with peers and later on intimate partner relationships, developing a sexual identity, learning to act economically and to deal with consumer and media offerings, and building up one's own value system, as well as political action capacity.

- In adulthood, it is normally expected to start a professional career, set up and manage a household, establish a family with children and provide care, cultivate friendships and social contacts and take responsibility as a citizen.

- Old age is about adapting to the changes in the physical and cognitive performance, shaping retirement from professional life, maintaining family relationships and finding a new role in the social network of friends and acquaintances, maintaining the role as economic and political citizen and preparing for the end of life.

The four groups of developmental tasks

The developmental tasks of the individual life stages build upon one another but present new challenges in each phase, which require a reorganisation of the personal and social resources. This reorganisation takes place at the biological-physical and the psychological level, the processing of the internal reality, as well as at the social and cultural level, the processing of the external reality.

Figure 3.1 gives an illustration of the position of developmental tasks within the overall framework of the model of productive processing of reality.

The individual developmental tasks can be assigned to four areas with quite similar requirements over the entire life course (Hurrelmann and Quenzel, 2013, p. 32):

1   *Qualifying*: The development of cognitive and social competences to exercise socially relevant activities. In an ideal case this means that school education and professional training, as well as the transition to a professional life are successfully completed and the role as a member of society exercising a professional activity can be fulfilled. This makes

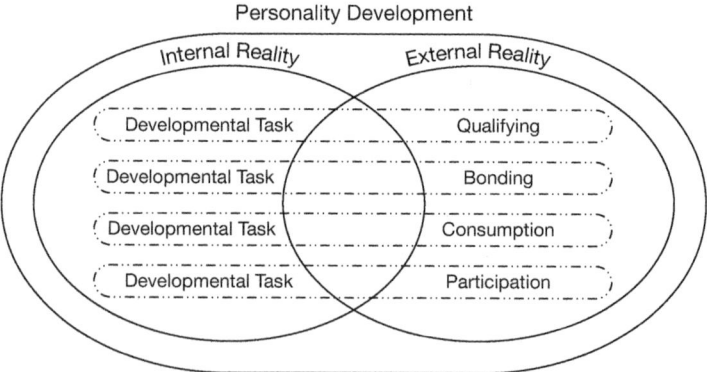

Figure 3.1 The position of developmental tasks within the overall framework of the model of productive processing of reality

it possible to finance an independent household as well as the 'economical reproduction' of one's own existence, and at the same time of the entire society.

2   *Bonding*: The development of gender and sexual identity, the emotional and social detachment from the parents, and later on the ability to intimately bond with a partner. If this developmental task is mastered, there is a basic willingness and ability to found a family with own children. This guarantees the 'biological reproduction' of the society.

3   *Consumption*: The development of motivation and relief strategies, as well as the ability to deal with economic, leisure and media offerings and the use of money. Basically, it is about preparing for the social role of consumer and economic citizen. If this developmental task is mastered, a person ideally has the ability to use consumer and leisure offerings to his or her own advantage, and to manage the own household. In addition, a successful 'psychological reproduction' is possible, meaning recreating the performance ability used up in other areas of life (education or profession) in a way that is beneficial to the individual as well as the society.

4   *Participation*: The development of a system of values and norms and the capacity for political participation. Basically, this means to accept the role as a citizen, to articulate own needs and interests and to be able to participate actively in public affairs. This requires the development of ethical, moral and political orientations and action competences based on these orientations.

Mastering these developmental tasks requires intensive 'work on the own personality' in each life stage. The physical changes, the psychological state and the social and ecological demands are perceived sensitively, taken into account in comparison with other people and balanced with the own needs and action plans. Flexible and resilient balancing structures between internal needs and external expectations are constantly developed. As previously mentioned, developmental tasks link the demands of internal and external reality with each other. For example the cognitive abilities must correspond with the choice of a school and profession, the physical conditions must match the requirements of work, the psychological and sexual orientations must be in harmony with the choice of a partner and the entertainment needs with the choice of leisure activities.

The tension between individuation and integration

The above-mentioned requirement of combining personal individuation and social integration and linking them with each other runs through all the developmental tasks. Individuation and integration are in a permanent state of tension during the entire life course. 'Individuation' means the development of an individual personality structure with distinctive physical, psychological and social characteristics and competences, as well as the subjective experience as a unique and singular personality. 'Integration' includes the respect for social values, norms and standards of conduct, the acceptance of social roles (the roles as a professional, founder of a family, consumer and political citizen) as well as integration in the social structures of society.

The combination of personal individuation and social integration is mainly discussed in the theory of psychosocial development by Erik H. Erikson (1964, 1968) and in the competence theory of Jürgen Habermas (1981/1984, 1981/1987). Through the subjective experience of individuation and integration, human beings realise the great difference between the requirements of the body and psyche on the one hand and the social and physical environment on the other. Most people become particularly aware of this tension and experience it with utmost sensitivity during puberty, when entering the stage of adolescence. For the first time during the life course, they have the ability in this development stage to consciously reflect about themselves, their own body, psyche and environment and realise that other people also have this ability.

The requirements of internal and external reality follow completely different rules and logics. The systems theory approaches of Talcott Parsons (1951) and Niklas Luhmann (1984/1995) emphasise these differences by pointing to the 'self-referential logics' of the systems body, psyche and society, which follow their own respective functions in order to maintain their structures, and which constitute foreign external worlds for each other. Particularly when a human being is thrown into a state of existential crisis (this includes puberty, accidents, blows of fate, economical and political crises, as well as severe illnesses), this can cause the feeling that the specific demands of internal and external reality can not be reconciled, as they involve completely different requirements.

Balancing individuation and integration as contradictory requirements and expectations can be an exhausting and agonising experience for a person because they are geared towards different directions. The gap between personal uniqueness and social community can cause a dissociative experience of the own reality. This can cause delays or blockages in the development of a self-identity. Also, the operative mode of productive processing of reality may be challenged to find new avenues (such as aggressive behaviour, depression, or drug use to escape reality) which are in opposition to a path pre-defined by developmental tasks to be coped with and mastered.

The formation of self-identity

If the developmental tasks are mastered, and the tensions between personal individuation and social integration connected with this process are successfully balanced, the formation of self-identity can take place. If the developmental tasks cannot be mastered, the formation of self-identity is jeopardised or even impossible. We can speak of self-identity if we see a continuity of self-experience in human beings based on a positive self-esteem and a feeling of self-efficacy over different stages of development and life phases. Although body and psyche undergo changes and social and psychological environmental conditions are different in each phase of life, human beings with a self-identity perceive themselves as the same personality. For human beings, self-identity is a precondition for the autonomous ability to act, for mental health and for successfully coping with life. If no self-identity is formed, all of these areas can be disrupted.

Beginning approximately in adolescence, it is possible for humans to perceive themselves as 'actors' on their own account and as 'objects' perceived by others. Accordingly, human beings can develop an image of themselves by analysing all the results of their previous perceptions and combining them into a 'self-image'. The self-image consists of subjective assessments that people have of themselves. The basis of this self-image is a realistic perception of the internal reality, meaning the genetic, physical and psychological potentials (especially the specific talents, the constitution and the temperament) and the possibilities to use these potentials to act in the external reality. If a person arrives at positive and optimistic assessments in this regard, he or she is able to develop a stable self-confidence and high self-esteem. According to the social learning theory of Bandura (1977), he or she develops a feeling of self-efficacy by ensuring that they are able to cope with the pending requirements effectively.

Requirements for successful coping

Disruptions in identity formation are mostly caused by a lack of congruity between the personal and social components of identity: the needs, motives and interests that aim at individuation on the one hand, and the social requirements that aim at integration on the other hand are not in a state of balance. This can lead to self-confidence disorders and subsequently to socially deviant and health-impairing behaviour. The more capable human beings are to make decisions and take action, the more abilities for coping with psychological and social problems they have, the more they are included in reliable social structures and networks and accepted in important social roles, the better the chances for self-identity, independent and autonomous action capacity and the possibilities for coping with life.

If the developmental tasks are successfully mastered, the tension between personal individuation and social integration can be balanced and a self-identity formed. As a consequence, the further personality development can take a normal course, and well-being and health can be achieved. If this is not successful, the tension between individuation and integration remains, and the identity is insecure. This can result in disturbances of the further personality development and problematic behaviour, which can lead to a physical–psychological imbalance and even illness.

Risks of unsuccessful coping

If developmental tasks are not successfully mastered, this causes different forms of problematic behaviour that constitute a risk for further personality development. When a person tries to cope with developmental tasks but does not succeed and suffers from the consequences, he or she will not be able to endure the resulting development pressure for long and will try to hide the failure out of self-protection and shame from the social environment.

Three risk paths

This can lead to three risk paths in coping with developmental tasks: an outward-oriented path, an avoiding path and an inward-oriented path:

- We can speak of an outward-oriented 'externalising' variation of unsuccessful coping with developmental tasks when a person reacts to the 'developmental pressure' that is created by aggression against others. The strong impairment of the self-esteem resulting from the failure to master one or several developmental tasks leads to an outward-oriented attitude.

- The second variation of a risk path in coping with developmental tasks is characterised by avoidance ('evading variant'). Hasty forms of behaviour express this 'leaving the field', in unsteady, changing social relationship patterns and danger of addiction, for example uncontrolled consumption of legal and illegal drugs, or food, and the excessive use of electronic media.

- In the inward-oriented, 'internalising' variation of coping behaviour, a person reacts to the development pressure with withdrawal and isolation, disinterest and apathy, psychosomatic disorders and depressive moods.

Particularly the theories of ecological development by Urie Bronfenbrenner (1979), of the production of one's own development by Richard L. Lerner (1976) and of salutogenesis by Aaron Antonovsky (1979) have contributed to these findings. These theories stress the analysis of the personal and the social resources available to a human being. This includes the individual action and communication skills, the basic abilities of role behaviour and the creative potentials of flexible action ('personal resources'), as well as the extent of material and immaterial support by the social environment ('social resources').

The availability of personal and social resources

Numerous and diverse personal and/or social resources create good conditions for coping successfully with developmental tasks. A lack of personal and social resources leads to a state of defencelessness that can be described as 'vulnerability', as a danger of helplessness. This condition arises in the case of critical events, such as accidents, death, or severe illness in the family. Under these circumstances, it is difficult to maintain the ability to cope with pending developmental tasks such as educational or professional performance because the resources are completely absorbed by the critical event. If a person is confronted with such events in disadvantageous financial situations, the coping capacity can be completely exhausted because the social resources do not provide for a 'safety net' that would enable the person to compensate for the loss of income and the additional psychological burdens. In most of the cases, such situations are aggravated by the inability to obtain access to adequate institutional support.

From the perspective of socialisation theory, it is necessary to master developmental tasks at least in a sufficient way in order to achieve a state of health. Positive self-esteem cannot be achieved without success in qualifying, bonding, the confident handling of the consumer world and media, and in establishing one's own value system. A deficit of mastering can result in various forms of health problems, whereas the successful coping with developmental tasks with their specific demands regarding the processing of the internal and external reality normally results in well-being and an increased joy of life. Crucial components of a health-promoting coping style are an optimistic attitude in addressing everyday challenges, the acceptance of one's own body and physical characteristics, the optimism to give the own life meaning, the possibility to influence the parameters important for one's own lifestyle and the confidence to shape one's own social and material environment (Antonovsky, 1979; Hurrelmann, 1989).

Unsuccessful coping can lead to a breakdown of active performance motivation and the ability to shape one's own life in a creative and enjoyable way. It is often expressed in health-detrimental patterns of diet, physical exercise, consumption, leisure activity, social engagement, political participation, professional activity, relationships, love and sexuality.

Here is one example from family research: When one parent becomes severely ill, the children often take on major caregiving and thus parental tasks. One can speak of the 'parentification' of the children, who are pushed into the role of an adult and often of a substitute partner without possessing the necessary resources to assume these roles. They set aside their own needs as a child and are pushed into 'reverse' role relationships. The pressure to adapt and cope, the fear of a breakdown of family, and a lack of support can lead to an inability to master their age-appropriate developmental tasks (educational performance, establishing contacts with friends and peers). This can lead to disruptions in their personality development. Sleep deficits and lapses in concentration, time constraints, learning difficulties and absence affect their everyday school life. The permanent violation of family norms leads to social isolation, fear and shame. Therefore, it is often difficult to ask for and make use of adequate institutional help (Beardslee, 2009).

Another example: children from refugee families (Fong, 2004) who come to another country at primary school age, who do not speak the main language in their country of immigration and must adapt to a completely foreign culture overnight. They inevitably fail in coping with the developmental task 'qualification' because of their enormous deficiencies in written language acquisition. This can quickly result in an inability to establish normal contacts with their classmates. These children are at risk to be identified as problematic and then expelled from school or relegated to a beginners' class. All of these disadvantages can escalate and cause discrimination along ethnic characteristics with xenophobic elements. The further personality development of these children can be permanently disrupted, particularly as it is difficult for them and their parents to find access to institutional support.

Complex requirements for the development of self-identity

As previously mentioned, wealthy democratic societies offer their members a greater variety of behavioural options than two or three generations ago, which leads to opportunities for personality development which are quite different from those in less developed societies. The sociologist Ulrich Beck (1992) pointed out that this constitutes a great chance for each individual member of society to choose the most important biographical options available that are suitable to their own personality and transfer them to their own life plan.

But this great degree of freedom must also be used, and this requires very specific competences. It is necessary to know one's own strengths and weaknesses well in order to negotiate an own lifestyle with the most important people within the social environment and to further develop it in a flexible manner, also under altered conditions. There is no 'master plan' on how to achieve this and hardly any examples or role models that can provide firm guidance. The responsibility for shaping the own biography and the criteria for the individual navigation through the life course lie in the hands of each and every individual person.

Today, a high degree of self-organisation is required in each phase of the life course in order to interconnect individuation and integration and establish a self-identity. This requires an accurate perception of the 'internal reality' of the physical and psychological resources in order to address the 'external reality' of the social and material conditions of life in an active manner. It can be assumed that self-identity is harder to achieve under the current living conditions than two or three generations ago. It must be developed repeatedly by permanently balancing the requirements of individuation and integration at each point of one's own life history. The de-standardisation of the requirements of life sets high standards for individuals to cope with these requirements.

No matter how challenging these demands may be, they carry the potential for a high degree of autonomy and originality in the personality development. Each individual stage of life involves the task of coordinating the distinct social living environments with their specific organisational requirements and still experience oneself as identical in these different worlds. If the developmental tasks are successfully mastered, this great variety of requirements can expand the scope of options and lead to a broad and varying range of autonomous actions. If not, this may result in the variants of problem behaviour mentioned above and hinder the formation of self-identity.

Questions

1. What is the definition of a developmental task?

2. What are the four areas of developmental tasks?

3. Why are personal individuation and social integration in a permanent state of tension during the entire life course?

4. What is the prerequisite for the formation of self-identity?

5. What are the three risk paths of unsuccessful coping with developmental tasks?

6. What are the complex requirements for the development of self-identity?

Answers

1   A developmental task describes the profile of individual action competences in dealing with the body, psyche and social and material environment, which is expected for a specific stage of life. Every person must manage this in his or her own individual way. Coping with these tasks requires a reconciliation of the biological and psychological requirements of internal reality with the social and ecological requirements of external reality.

2   The four areas of developmental tasks:

   - *Qualifying*: The development of the competences that are necessary to assume the role of a member of society exercising a professional activity.

   - *Bonding*: The development of physical and gender identity, the emotional and social detachment from the parents, and later on the ability to intimately bond with a partner.

   - *Consumption*: The development of motivation and relief strategies, as well as the ability to deal with economic, leisure and media offerings, and the use of money.

   - *Participation*: The development of a system of values and norms and the capacity for political participation.

3   The tension is inevitable, because individuation means the development of an individual personality structure with distinctive physical, psychological and social characteristics and competences, as well as the subjective experience as a unique and singular personality. Integration is based on the respect for social values, norms and standards of

conduct, the acceptance of social roles (the roles as a professional, founder of a family, consumer and political citizen) as well as acceptance of the social structures of society.

4   The formation of self-identity can take place as soon as the developmental tasks are mastered and the tensions between personal individuation and social integration are successfully balanced. Self-identity is the state of a continuity of self-experience based on a positive self-esteem and a feeling of self-efficacy over different stages of the life course.

5   The three risk paths of unsuccessful coping with developmental tasks:

  • An outward-oriented 'externalising' variation of unsuccessful coping with developmental tasks is when a person reacts to the 'developmental pressure' by aggression against others.

  • The 'evading' variation is expressed by hasty forms of behaviour, in unsteady, changing social relationship patterns and danger of addiction, for example uncontrolled consumption of legal and illegal drugs, or food, and the excessive use of electronic media.

  • In the inward-oriented, 'internalising' variation of coping behaviour, a person reacts to the development pressure with withdrawal and isolation, disinterest and apathy, psychosomatic disorders and depressive moods.

6.   Modern democratic societies offer their members a greater variety of behavioural options than traditional societies three or more generations ago, which leads to a broad spectrum of opportunities for personality development.

There is no 'master plan' on how to achieve this, and hardly any examples or role models that can provide firm guidance. The responsibility for shaping the own biography and the criteria for the individual navigation through the life course lie in the hands of each and every individual person.

4

Productive processing of reality during the life course

Increased longevity and the changing social and economical conditions have altered the structure of the life course and the sequence of the individual life stages. Childhood is becoming ever shorter because the onset of puberty is occurring at an increasingly earlier stage in the life course and with it, adolescence. At the same time, adolescence is prolonged by an extended phase of education and vocational training. Adolescents need more time to master developmental tasks before taking on their occupational, familial, consumer and citizen roles that are characteristic for adulthood. At the end of life, more and more people are experiencing an extended senior phase.

This provides more opportunities for a creative and open 'production' of the own personality in each life phase. Already during childhood, there are many opportunities for shaping one's own personality due to the direct access to the media and the leisure and consumer markets; in addition, most children already have their own financial resources available. During adolescence, the possibilities for self-organisation of the personality further increase. The open character of this life stage as transitional phase between childhood and adulthood offers great margins for an individualistic and self-responsible lifestyle

(Arnett, 2014). Since adolescents often live in situations with uncertain outcomes and uncertain perspectives for the future, they are forced to establish individual target prospects and give their life meaning in order to achieve a minimum of stability in their everyday world (e.g. in phases of transition from school to professional life, or when a friendship or partnership ends). Basically, the same applies to the life stages adulthood and 'seniorhood'.

Due to increased longevity and the great margins for an individual lifestyle, personality development is never really completed in any life stage but is in a state of constant progress. Therefore, for many people the search and sound attitude characteristic for adolescence also remains a pattern and model for personality development in subsequent life stages.

Personality development during the life course

The key statement of the model of productive processing of reality in socialisation theory that can be derived from these explanations is that personality development continues during the entire life course. The life course is subdivided into consecutive life stages with specific developmental tasks. Due to the changing economical, social and cultural conditions, human beings are faced with the challenge of redefining their biographical and societal position in every respective life stage. Due to increased longevity and the great margins that are typical for today's individual lifestyle, there is a seamless transition between the individual life stages. Therefore, although the fundamental basis is established during childhood and adolescence, personality development is never completed but remains in constant progress, with more or less significant boosts.

This core statement is based on the psychological theories of developmental tasks by Robert J. Havighurst (1953), the theory of self-production by Richard L. Lerner (1976) and the theory of stages of development by Erik H. Erikson (1964, 1968). Among the sociological theories, especially the competence theory of Jürgen Habermas (1981/1984, 1981/1987) and the theory of social construction by Peter L. Berger and Thomas Luckmann (1966) attach particular importance to the life course. Pierre Bourdieu's (1980/1990) concept of habitus also underlines the importance of experiences and knowledge, which build upon each other and lead to a cohesive perception of the personality and a coherent schema of perception, thought and action.

Changes in the life course during the past century

Within one century, from 1900 to the present, economic and social changes, in particular a constant increase in wealth, the extension of education and vocational training periods and the ongoing improvement of working conditions, have led to a noticeable structural change of the life course with direct effects for the sequence and character of the individual life stages, and with it for the profile of the respective developmental tasks. Taking the three dates 1900, 1950 and 2000 as symbolic landmarks, the change of the typical structural characteristics of the life course with division into different life stages can be illustrated as shown in Figure 4.1.

As the illustration shows, in 1900 the life course in highly developed societies only consisted of the stages childhood and adulthood. The transition from childhood to adulthood mostly coincided with the transition to professional life and the founding of a family. The end of adulthood already occurred

Phases of the Life Course Historical Comparison

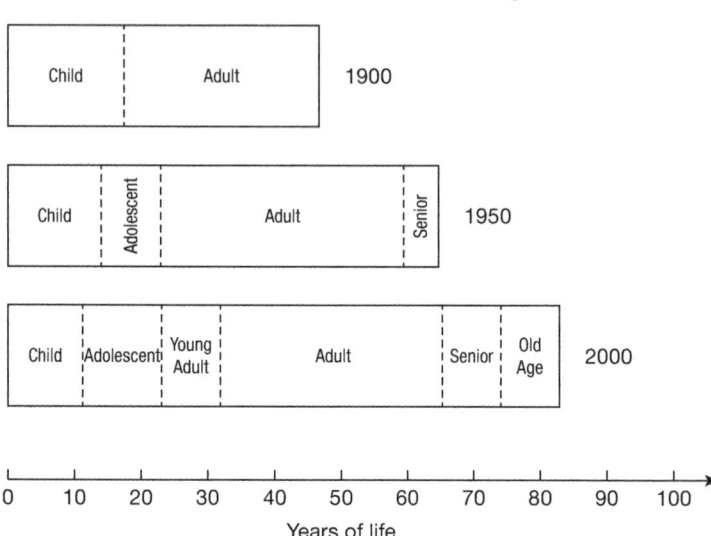

Figure 4.1 Phases of the life course in historical comparison

during the course of professional life, with a relatively early death by today's standards at the age of about 50.

In 1950, longevity had increased significantly. The life stages adolescence and seniorhood had developed anew. Due to the earlier onset of puberty, childhood was shorter than in 1900 and adolescence served as a transitional phase from the dependent state of childhood to the independent state of adulthood. Adulthood was considerably extended by increased longevity. Therefore, the entire life course was dominated by the professional and family life of adulthood. After withdrawing from professional life, it became possible to live out a short retirement relieved from the obligations of adulthood.

In 2000, longevity increased once again and the life course was subdivided even more than in 1950. The life phase childhood shortened to just about 12 years and adolescence extended considerably into early adulthood. The life stage 'late adolescence', also described as 'early adulthood', had emerged in which the professional life has not yet started and a family not yet been founded. This entailed a delayed transition to professional and family life. Adulthood remained dominant for shaping the life course but was more subdivided than in 1950 due to an increase of professional and familial disruptions and restarts. The life stage seniorhood extended to a total period of 15 years, and in its first phase was no longer characterised by rest but instead by a variety of activities that are typical for adulthood before transitioning into the final phase of old age.

The biographical sequencing of the life course

As the figure shows, until the middle of the past century, most members of society lived a sequence of life stages with fixed rules and expectations, and clear transitions. The society supported social integration in each of the life stages and facilitated biographical planning accordingly. Biographical expectations and cultural as well as legal regulations were harmonised.

This is most clearly reflected by the typical life course around 1950: it consists of three parts, preparing for a profession (childhood and adolescence), exercising the profession (adulthood) and retiring from professional responsibilities (seniorhood). Childhood was dedicated to the development of the basic structures of personality, and adolescence to the preparation for full membership in society as a gainfully employed person and founder of a family. Adulthood was the biographical zenith of life and provided status and security and was followed by the phase of retirement and successive withdrawal from social responsibility.

57

This structure of the life course made it possible to develop a predictable sequenced biography. Society offered its members the possibility of a 'standardised' life course. This was connected with a uniform pattern of lifestyle. Each member of society had recourse to a meaningful biographical rhythm of the life course, in a certain sense a standard biography that was shared by all members of society and which could only lose structure as a result of severe economic crises or political upheavals, or – at the individual level – by severe illness or unemployment. Otherwise, the biography was standardised.

The pattern of the standard biography of the twentieth century

This standard biography of the twentieth century consisted of three stages in the life course based on the following biographical ideas:

1   During the infant period, until approximately the age of 6, the child lives in the sheltered environment of the family and can develop the most important action competences and personal abilities. During the following school years, intellectual and technical competences are trained and symbolically documented by graduation. With graduation, adolescence is completed and the transition to adulthood fulfilled.

2   Adult status is realised with the start of professional training and the gainful employment that follows. In addition, the detachment from the family of origin takes place together with the transition to adulthood and, as a rule, a family is founded. The adult status is assigned to each individual over a long active lifespan until retirement. During this period,

human beings are full members of society and also assume the relevant economic and political responsibility for shaping the economic, social and cultural conditions of life in the community.

3   With retirement, the cultural and legal withdrawal from gainful employment and the transition to seniorhood is initiated, which extends until death. This phase is seen as a time of rest and thus a well-deserved period during which the individual is relieved from the tasks and responsibilities of adulthood.

Such a 'standard' biography was considered 'natural' until well into the 1980s. It is illustrated in Figure 4.2.

Those who deviated from it were socially marginalised. This was for example the case for women without children who did

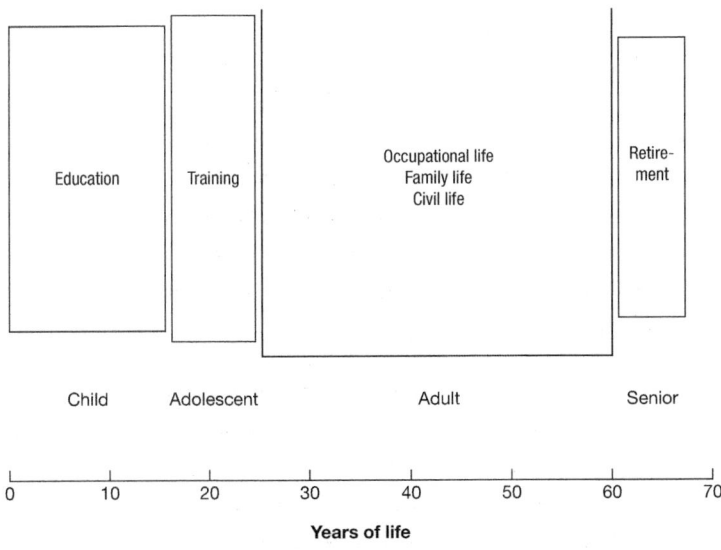

Figure 4.2 The standard biography of the twentieth century

not want or were unable to found a family and for men who were not gainfully employed. The standard biography applied to members of all social classes, but also included significant differences between men and women. Since women were as mothers responsible for the children's education, they were not supposed to work during the life stage of adulthood. This was reserved for men, who were at the same time expected to be the 'bread-winners' for the entire family.

Institutional backup for the standard biography

The patterns of standard biography were established by a series of political, legal and institutional regulations:

- For the stage of childhood, domestic education by the mother as 'housewife' was considered as standard by a large segment of the population and in politics. The corresponding financial and legal regulations (e.g. tax benefits and the social acceptance of the 'housewife' status) stabilised the respective family constellation.

- The institutions school, professional training institution and university provided the formal framework for the phase of adolescence, whereas the young generation without formal qualifications remained largely excluded from the labour market with the possibility to earn one's own money.

- The labour market was seen as the institutional basis for a man's phase of adulthood. Women were responsible for the private household, raising children and the cultivation of contacts within the family and in the neighbourhood. Their working husbands, in turn, financially secured women. The family received child benefits and other state benefits to compensate for the disadvantages, as compared to childless professionals.

- Social welfare facilities and legal constructions of insurance supported and secured the retirement age with a calculable pension. It was often not possible to work longer than the legal retirement age, even if a person was able and willing.

The gradual break up of the standard biography

All of these regulations and the concepts of a 'normal' lifestyle behind them continue to have an impact today and are partly still in place, although it already became clear at the end of the 1980s that the three-part structured life course would change and can only be realised in exceptional cases. The reason for this is the profound changes to the economic and social framework conditions, which involve new requirements for the sequencing of the life course:

- The professional requirements and working conditions changed to the effect that they require an ever longer and highly qualifying education. Through rationalisation and automation processes, and the worldwide interdependence of economies, the number of jobs cannot increase infinitely, which means that jobs are not available to all members of the young generation. As a result, a large segment of the young generation finds access to employment only very late or not at all. In addition, fixed-term employment is often the norm, which makes it difficult or even impossible to found a family.

- The desires and perspectives for personal life have changed. People in all stages of life strive to freely develop their individual abilities. This is true for both genders. In an open democratic society, only few women and men want to live according to the division of labour connected with the standard biography, which still seemed natural in 1950. More and more women, also mothers, want to participate in professional life. Because women, just like men, must go through a long period of education, founding a family is often delayed.

- In today's materially affluent societies, there are greater opportunities throughout the life course to realise ideas of life, which do not necessarily fit the traditional patterns. For example it is possible to start a company at age 17 or to work in a corporation as a 75-year-old pensioner. There are hardly any restrictions left regarding the personal life style, for example in partnerships. This development has suspended the traditional rhythm for shaping the life course, which was still considered to be natural in 1950.

Today, the individual life stages no longer follow each other in clearly defined sequences but can also overlap and merge. A fixed sequence of school and professional education and subsequent employment is no longer guaranteed. Some young people have the opportunity to enter employment and live an adult life according to traditional patterns already while attending school or during their studies, whereas others may encounter unpredictable situations and uncertainties due to long periods of unemployment and fixed-term employment contracts, even at the adult age. This may lead to insecurity and the fear to establish a permanent relationship and found a family.

The pattern of the multi-biography of the twenty-first century

Because the margins for an individual lifestyle have continually increased, the transitions between childhood, adolescence, adulthood and seniorhood have become fluent. This goes hand in hand with a significantly higher demand to shape one's own life independently from, and partly even in tension with, social, legal and institutional rules and regulations. In each phase of life, every person is faced with the challenge to permanently cope with uncertainties and unpredictable situations, with all their positive and negative surprises. This has become characteristic for highly developed, globally connected societies. Trying and learning, living with provisional arrangements, and enduring tensions between contradictory expectations – these action patterns and attitudes, which were previously typical only for adolescence are indispensable today in each stage of life. This applies to education and professional life, as well as for leisure time and personal life. As a result, the standard biography of the twentieth century was remodelled into a 'multi-biography' of the twenty-first century.

The biographical composition of the life course of the twenty-first century is illustrated in Figure 4.3.

As shown in this figure, the transition to the traditional stage of gainful employment and family life is postponed in the life course. The life stages solely characterised by education and preparation for professional life are normally completed around the age of 25. Afterwards, many young people continue their general and professional education, but it is interrupted or accompanied by occasional jobs. Cohabitation in personal life and completely autonomous action patterns in the areas of consumption, media and leisure time can lead to a lifestyle that

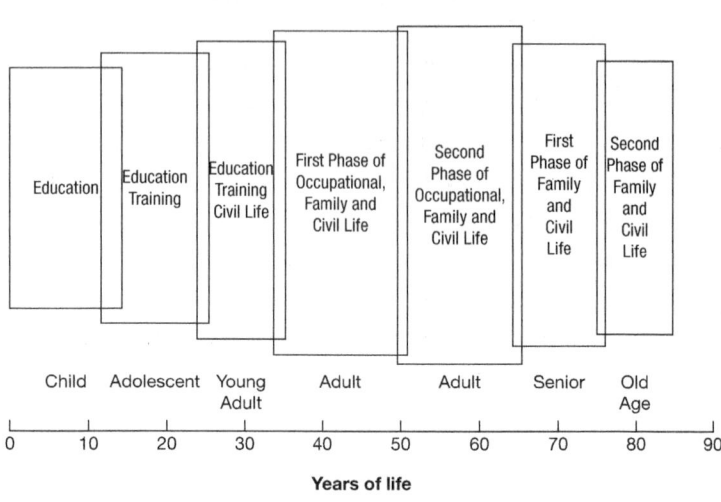

Figure 4.3 The multi-biography of the twenty-first century

has nothing in common with the traditional stage of adolescence during the 1950s and takes on characteristics of adulthood.

The belated transition to the roles of adulthood creates a flexible transitional period between adolescence and adulthood. It constitutes a biographical 'moratorium', which serves personal development without the restrictions of professional life or family responsibilities and child education. During this phase, a flexible and creative combination of education, profession and private life is possible.

The loss or change of employment or the loss or change of a partner often makes diverse reorientations possible and necessary during adulthood. After the first phase of professional and family life, many people experience a 'second adulthood' around the age of 50 or 55, with a new partnership and a new family life, often also with a new career. This is depicted in Figure 4.3 under the label of 'occupation, family, and civil life A and B'.

64

The transition to seniorhood also becomes fluent in this context. The traditional image of 'retirement' with a complete withdrawal from professional and family life no longer fits; instead, an active lifestyle with occasional jobs and volunteer activities has become characteristic for this phase. The opportunities to shape biographical details are often no longer distinguishable from those of (early) adulthood. During the last life stage, a phase of 'un-rest' is also possible for many elderly people. The traditional standard biography concept, in which old age is characterised by retreat and withdrawal from active life, only becomes reality at the very end of life ('old ager').

High demands on biographical management

It is characteristic for highly developed, complex societies to offer their members very little support in the transition from one life stage to the next. Basically, every person is responsible for his or her own 'biography management' and has to select appropriate stimuli from different institutions of the external reality:

• Elementary support is provided within families and among friends and peers. Families, however, have great difficulties in preparing for today's typically more flexible sequencing of the life course. They are small in size and unable to offer all the experiences that are necessary to cope with educational, occupational, economic and organisational requirements of everyday life. Friends and peers to a certain degree compensate for these deficits, but because of their fluid and loosely coupled network structure, their influence also is limited.

- Traditional socialisation institutions such as schools and institutions of occupational training stick narrowly to their core functions and hardly focus on providing their students with the competences needed for the transition to the independent role as founder of a family and part of the workforce.

- Firms, corporations and companies follow commercial dynamics and hardly consider the social integration of the people working with them, such as their responsibilities regarding the education of children. This makes it difficult to harmonise family life and gainful employment.

- The social security systems provide some incentives, which do not exactly correspond with the organisation of a consistent lifestyle concept. The pension fund sometimes encourages early retirement, even if the intellectual and physical power of a person is sufficient to continue his or her career.

- The mass media provide a multitude of information and entertainment, but no tailored advice for an individual lifestyle.

This broad spectrum of socialisation contexts and societal institutions makes it difficult for people in all stages of life to harmonise their biographical expectations and individual concepts of life with the social standards. The demanding challenge of mastering the developmental tasks and balancing individuation and integration has to be mastered one's own responsibility, and accordingly, the requirements of developing and safeguarding the self-identity are very high.

Demographic change and intergenerational relationships

With increasing longevity, the share of elderly people among the population constantly increases, while the share of younger people is considerable lower due to decreasing birth rates since the mid-1960s.

Change in the age structure

This demographic trend has greatly altered the 'age pyramid' that has been characteristic for western industrial societies since approximately 1900, which now has a very high percentage of younger and a low percentage of older people. Today, the population structure looks more like a tree than a pyramid because the young generation no longer constitutes the largest among the three population groups but is now the smallest. Children and adolescents are in the minority among the three generations; the age group of 45 and over and seniors form the majority.

Due to their increasing demographic weight, a growing portion of tax revenue and compensation payments is earmarked for adults and seniors. Most highly developed countries in Europe have a well-developed system of transfer payments for social assistance, unemployment, occupational disability, illness and retirement that mainly benefits middle-aged and elderly people, with only a few exceptions. The pension insurance, which is quite good in many countries, is of symbolic importance for the guaranteed coverage of claims to social resources allocated to the older generation after retirement from an active professional life. It is particularly significant that a legal claim to all of these payments exists that is to a great extent independent from political influence due to an insurance model that has been collectively agreed upon.

The importance of intergenerational relationships

In comparison, the younger generation enjoys much less security regarding their future financial situation. Important resources for children and adolescents, particularly for their education and training, are dependent upon the state's economic and financial situation and not stabilised by automatic adjustment or insurance regulations. Basically, the welfare policies in most of the highly developed western countries are designed in a way to preserve the status quo of those groups who are already part of the working population or have retired. In contrast, those population groups who have not yet acquired a social status are the ones who are structurally neglected, and this applies of course to children and adolescents.

In the medium-term, this imbalance in the distribution of resources can lead to political conflicts between the younger, the middle and the older generation. The younger generation will react sensitively to their structural disadvantages at the latest when it comes to economic crises which prevent their access to the labour market and thereby to social security benefits (Lehmann, 2005). As soon as adolescents feel insecure regarding their future perspectives, this leads to political protests and a noticeable reserve towards democratic institutions, such as parties and parliaments. These attitudes have been observed particularly in socially disadvantaged groups of members of the young generation (as confirmed by the German Youth Study, Shell Deutschland, 2015).

A preferential treatment of the population groups who have already acquired a social status can lead to stagnation in further social and economic development. It is usually the younger generation who stimulates and advances social decisions and in doing so, breaks up old structures that are no longer useful in view of the changed economic and social conditions. However, to be able to fulfil their role as driving force, the young generation needs strong socialisation and education agents that promote their potentials in the best possible way. If a society does not provide adequate resources in this regard, its existence will be jeopardised in the long-term.

Questions

1   What kind of changes have occurred in the life course during the past century and what are the reasons?

2   What are the differences between the 'standard biography' of the twentieth century and the complex 'multi-biography' of the twenty-first century?

3   Why are the demands on biographical management so high today?

4   What are the risks of the demographic transition by which the share of elderly people among the population constantly increases, while the share of younger people is decreasing?

Answers

1   Until today, the life phase childhood shortened to just about 12 years, and adolescence extended considerably into early adulthood. Adulthood remains dominant for shaping the life course but is subdivided due to an increase of professional and familial disruptions and restarts. The life stage seniorhood extends to a total period of 15 years, and in its first phase is no longer characterised by rest but instead by a variety of cultural, political and civil activities before transitioning into the phase of very old age. The demographic aging of the population, the prolonged extension of life, economic and social changes such as a constant increase in wealth, the extension of education and vocational training periods and the ongoing improvement of working conditions have led to these noticeable structural changes of the life course.

2   In the standard biography, the individual life stages have a clearly defined function and follow each other in sequences without really overlapping and merging. A fixed sequence of school and professional education, subsequent employment and parenthood, and finally retirement from employment and active family life is the rule. In the multi-biography, an overlap and merging of life stages is possible. For example, some young people have the opportunity to enter employment and live an adult life according to traditional patterns already while attending school or during their studies, whereas others may encounter long periods of unemployment until the adult age. This may lead to insecurity and the postponement of establishing a permanent relationship and found a family. In each of the stages of life, an individual has a multitude of options for shaping the life course.

3   It is characteristic for highly developed societies to offer their members a multitude of options but no or only very little support in the transition from one stage of life to the next. Basically, every person is responsible for his or her own 'biography management'. This opens up lots of new possibilities and potentials, but at the same time makes it difficult for people in all stages of life to harmonise their biographical expectations and individual concepts of life with the social opportunities and standards. The task of balancing individuation and integration is an integral part of the biography management, and accordingly, the requirements of developing and safeguarding the self-identity are very high.

4   An imbalance in the distribution of resources can lead to political conflicts between the younger, the middle and the older generation. The younger generation will react sensitively to their structural disadvantages at the latest when it comes to economic crises, which prevent their access to the labour market and thereby to social security benefits. As soon as adolescents feel insecure regarding their future perspectives, this leads to political protests and a noticeable reserve towards democratic institutions, such as parties and parliaments.

CHAPTER 5

Socialisation in the individual life stages

The explanations in the previous chapter show how much the individual stages of the life-course have shifted and changed in their extent and form over the past 100 years. Some of the challenges resulting from this restructuring of the life course for the biographic organisation and socialisation have already been mentioned. Today, a very open form of the life course is predominant, which enables a 'chosen biography' but also requires a demanding 'biography management'. As has been shown, the implementation of such a biography management often fails today due to a lack of personal competences, but also due to persisting traditional, social, legal and institutional regulations stemming from the era of the alleged standard biography.

This chapter will discuss the critical demands for the productive processing of internal and external reality in the individual life stages of childhood, adolescence, adulthood and seniorhood. Particular account is taken of the differences according to social background. It aims at identifying the structural problems occurring in coping with the developmental tasks to be mastered in the respective stages. This is done on the basis of the classification of developmental tasks in four groups described above: 'Qualifying', the task of developing the competences necessary to cope with the social and performance requirements, as well as for later professional tasks; 'bonding', the task of accepting the physical development and gender identity, and establishing partner relationships; 'consumption', the task of developing the abilities required for dealing with the economic, leisure and media markets; and 'participation', the task of developing a system of values and norms required to assert one's own interests and participate in shaping the community.

Coping with developmental tasks in the life stage childhood

Until the nineteenth century, the differentiation between the life stages childhood, adolescence and adulthood did not exist. Society did not provide children a sheltered social or psychological environment exclusively reserved for their education and training. Instead, at a young age they already lived and worked in family-owned businesses, just like the adults, and wore the same clothes, performed the same tasks and saw and heard the same things. They were perceived and treated as 'small adults'. As a rule, the specific needs of children were not safeguarded. Many children had to bear significant burdens, exploitation and abuse (Bühler-Niederberger, 2016; Qvortrup, Corsaro and Honig, 2009).

This situation only changed in the nineteenth century, when the industrialisation process brought about an increasing separation of work and family life. Children now lived in families that were shielded from economic production and regarded as education agents. Kindergartens, schools and other public educational institutions that considered their task as promoting the personality development of the young generation and preparing children and adolescents for life in the society supported them. Their influence has steadily increased during the past decades.

Problems in coping with developmental tasks

Which problems can occur today in coping with the developmental tasks of the life stage childhood? As explained in the previous chapter, this life stage has become ever shorter due to the very early start of puberty. Accordingly, we see an accumulation of demands regarding the processing of internal and external reality in a short period.

- **Developmental task qualifying:** Today, the seriousness of performance pressure is part of childhood and begins with compulsory school attendance at age 6. Even at the preschool age, many children sense their parents' expectation of a rapid advancement of their cognitive and intellectual development in order to prepare for the performance demands of school. They are confronted with the developmental task 'qualifying' with nearly the same intensity as adolescents. They are firmly taught that they live in a competitive society and that their first steps along the path to professional competence are decisive for their chances during the entire future life course. The margin for a playful childhood with sufficient time for detours in the personal development is therefore extremely limited.

- **Developmental task bonding:** The parental home clearly remains the most important agent of socialisation during childhood. Mother and father play the key role for all aspects of personality development. However, children today must also be prepared for changes to the family constellation at any time. One out of three children experiences a break down in parental relationships; these children are then required to cope with the tensions resulting from these changes, and possibly with a new relationship of one of the parents. The social ties in the family have loosened overall. This enables adults to enter into and live in flexible forms of partnerships but this can also violate the children's needs for community and belonging. Ultimately, children are always the 'appendages' of their parents' partnerships and thus affected by their insecurity and instability without being able to play a role in shaping them.

- **Developmental task consumption:** In the areas of consumption and leisure time, children, as well as adolescents and adults experience the advantages and disadvantages of a modern, democratic, open and commercially oriented society. Especially in the use of media, they are able to move more or less freely and are to some extent more proficient in using information and communication technologies than their parents. They are 'digital natives', because interactive media constitutes their natural environment. But this also includes the challenge to process the contents that comes with it. Even children must be able to follow and evaluate news about social, political and ecological developments in the world today, including crises and catastrophes. The great number of stimuli in the leisure sector leads to overstimulation and increasing expectations regarding the various forms of entertainment, diversion and an exciting crossing of limits. This can impede the realistic judgment of events, as well the development of a structured self-image and worldview.

- **Developmental task participation:** Children experience the diversity of their environment also by communicating with people from other cultures, regions and religions. Children feel the cultural and social tensions in everyday social life through their friendships, which are established step by step starting at the primary school age and influence their leisure behaviour and media habits. They experience the differences between people of different religions and beliefs. Their attention is also drawn to the increasing gap between rich and poor at an early stage, especially because many of them are affected themselves by their parents' relative poverty and must live in unfavourable living and environmental conditions. Overall, the opportunities to actively shape their living environment remain minimal.

Thus, childhood today means living in insecure social relationships and in a competitive society in which only individual performance counts. Childhood also means to live in a world with a leisure market that is characterised by consumption and commercial stimuli, to experience the increasing shortage of play areas and open spaces in the living environment and to learn that the ecological environment can be harmful (e.g. noise and environmental pollution in the neighbourhood, or chemically treated food). Finally, childhood also means the experience of hardly having the chance to actively influence these processes.

Coping with developmental tasks in the life stage adolescence

The life stage adolescence includes the period between puberty and the entrance into an independent professional and family life that can be equated with adulthood. Like no other life stage, adolescence stands for the tension between personal individuation and social integration. Adolescents must be able to cope with their physical and psychological characteristics at a time in which they are under great pressure to socially integrate, particularly in school performance and professional education (Petersen, Koller, Motti-Stefanidi and Verma, 2017).

The outstanding feature of the socialisation process in adolescence is the development of a self-identity, which is for the first time possible in this phase. It requires an adequate self-image in line with the respective age and developmental stage, thus a realistic assessment of the personal and social resources. A precondition for the development of a self-image is the ability to differentiate between one's own person with one's own internal reality and the surrounding external reality. This ability is developed during the course of adolescence. The reflexive relationship of a human being with the own body and his or her needs, motives and interests becomes more differentiated and complex, and reaches a qualitatively new development stage in early adolescence. The same applies for the assessment of the social and material conditions of the environment.

Today, adolescents are expected to live a creative and individual lifestyle in order to balance the enormous tensions between the potentials of independence in various life areas. Such a lifestyle seems to be possible especially if the life stage adolescence is not interpreted in a traditional way, as a transitional phase from childhood to complete adulthood, but as a life stage that is shaped independently and has a special quality. The division of adolescence into the first phase until about age 20, which is mainly dedicated to education and training, and a second phase until about age 30–35, which allows a free lifestyle in the areas of qualification, bonding, consumption and participation, expresses this attitude.

What are the typical challenges today in coping with the developmental tasks of the life stage adolescence?

- **Developmental task qualification:** This task places great demands on adolescents today. The high performance expectations that already exist in childhood further increase and are experienced as strong pressure by many adolescents. Today, high-level education and training qualifications have become necessary but by no means sufficient prerequisites for acceptance in the professional world during times of job shortages and international competition. Therefore, a basic condition for coping with the developmental tasks in this area is the ability to deal with the uncertainty of actually advancing to the stage of adulthood and becoming a full member of society, or having to remain in the moratorium-like state of adolescence. Adolescents must be able to withstand the structural uncertainty of not knowing whether they will be able to obtain a long-term professional position in the future, only short-term work opportunities, or even work at all. As this is decisive for the decision to found a family, the biographical uncertainty they must deal with increases even further.

- **Developmental task bonding:** The life stage of adolescence is still perceived as a preparatory phase for the independent state of adulthood as regards sexuality, partnership and family life. However, the prerequisites and framework conditions for this transition have become more liberal and informal when compared to earlier generations. Adolescents are largely free to shape their friendships, partnerships and sexual relationships, and develop a lifestyle with a relatively high degree of independence, similar to adults. In contrast to earlier generations, cohabitation in an intimate partnership is possible for many years without founding a family.

Adolescence must be considered as a life stage in which severe personal crises occur. Young women and men in puberty show extremely sensitive reactions to the physical and psychological changes they are facing, but also to the challenges they are suddenly confronted with in their social and material environment. It is a particularly conflict-prone period in which a number of 'adolescence crises' must be mastered. The related tensions and mood swings must be experienced to the full extent to develop a mature personality structure and the ability to balance the requirements of individuation and identity and establish an efficient self-identity. Only after having endured these crises is it possible to overcome a merely superficial adaptation to social norms and cultural environment, with a mechanical performance orientation and materialistic motivations towards money, status and career, and to develop autonomous action competences.

During the period of adolescence, the demand to balance personal individuation and social integration and to develop one's own personal and social identity on this basis intensifies. In today's living conditions, the chances of developing one's own personal identity are very good because traditional rules for behavioural roles and the corresponding value orientations are no longer valid, and individuals can choose from a great variety of opportunities to find their own solutions for everyday tasks and problems. On the other hand, it is difficult to find a social identity because the possibilities for assuming social responsibility are relatively limited; in addition to this, the transition to the recognised economic status of a gainfully employed person important for the development of social identity is delayed more and more. Accordingly, the challenge for today's adolescents to master the task of developing a self-identity with the two components of personal and social identity has become greater.

- **Developmental task consumption:** An even greater variety of offers by the media and leisure world is available to adolescents than to children, and even more so because they usually have the required financial resources to use them. But the mainly commercially controlled media offerings require a well-structured concept of how to use them; otherwise, they can lead to ecstatic consumption patterns and a danger of addiction. In such cases, adolescents are not in full control of their use of such offerings but get caught up with them and are unable to steer temporal extent or the social consequences. This danger also exists especially during adolescence with regard to psychoactive drugs, which are consumed to enhance perception and sensation.

  For the self-determined use of media and leisure offerings, adolescents need an inner classification system with a built-in 'relevance compass' in order to flexibly and reasonably cope with the great variety of action requirements and the contradictions in the granting of personal autonomy. In a highly individualistic society, it is important to instinctively know where they are headed and where they see their position within the society in the long-term. If they have a stable self-identity, they have the best conditions to use the available scope to their advantage without facing the risk of having their personal needs and desires controlled by the dynamics of media and leisure offers.

- **Developmental task participation:** Adolescents require a sensitive grasp of the difficulties of future planning, especially in regard to such risks as unemployment, environ-

83

mental pollution, health hazards and threat of war. They must learn to live with the 'fear' of not knowing whether they will actually be able to live a life worth living, and whether the world will still be inhabitable for them. Despite all these worries and concerns, they will only be able to cope with their developmental tasks if they are convinced of their self-efficacy, or in other words, are confident enough to master the requirements of their life despite all the adverse circumstances.

In a democratic society, they have the possibility to assert their interests and to participate politically, but they must repeatedly decide if it is worth the effort. The changing (and overall decreasing) participation of adolescents in environmental protection and civil rights movements today shows that political participation is competing with other lifestyle preferences (professional orientation, consumption).

Coping with developmental tasks in the life stage adulthood

Since modern, individualistic societies grant so many margins for unconventional action patterns, adults today are not confronted with as much friction and resistance as was the case during the era of the 'standard biography'. Due to the relatively early independence in the areas of consumption, media and partnerships on the one hand, and the long period of education and training with economic dependence on the other, the transitional period from adolescence to adulthood comes very late today and must be shaped in a biographically meaningful manner by each individual. This has lots of repercussions for coping with the developmental tasks.

What are the typical challenges today in coping with the developmental tasks of the life stage adult?

- **Developmental task qualifying:** The life stage of adulthood is traditionally defined by assuming the role of breadwinner and founding a family. As a result of the extended life stage of adolescence, both of these social milestones are now occurring at very different points in time. As such, the onset of the life stage adulthood is occurring much later in life. Due to an increasing share of the population who do not live in marital relationships and an increase in unemployment, some members of society do not even reach the status of adult in the sense of the standard biography. This clearly shows how significantly this restructuring of the life course has also changed the character of the most important life stage (Wanberg, 2012).

  The transition to adulthood usually occurs for the majority of the population between the ages of 25 and 30 and requires a great deal of self-organisation. Adulthood has not remained unaffected by the precarious economic conditions of the last few decades. Interrupted or even abandoned careers during periods of mass unemployment prove to be challenging for biography management in the life stage mature adulthood, which affects growing numbers of professionals. This creates a necessity for occupational retraining, a change of jobs and continuing education and vocational training – demands that were atypical just a generation ago.

- **Developmental task bonding:** Every transition which takes place during adulthood requires that the self-image is reorganised and defined anew, which usually goes hand in hand with balancing earlier experiences and anticipating those to come, much as in the adolescent years. A marked break occurs between the ages of 45 and 50, at which time the zenith of physical and mental strength is achieved. This break offers many people a suitable opportunity to compare the aspirations, perspectives and desires they have set for their professional and private lives with those they have actually achieved and with those they can realistically achieve in the future. This comparison can especially lead to a midlife crisis when people realise that they are unable to achieve these professional and personal goals in the way they had hoped.

This midlife balancing process can thus become a great burden and create even more stress if the children of the family, who usually detach and become independent during this period, have also not attained the starting position in school and occupation desired by the parents. Many adults are pushed into a sandwich position through their middle status in the family generation line-up, which allows them intensive contact to their children as well as to the parent-grandparent generation. The sandwich position can go hand in hand with the obligation to provide social and psychological support not only for the young but also for the old generation at the same time. This constellation occurs for example when the own children are still in kindergarten or are of school age and need intense guidance, and at the same time the own parents (and possibly grandparents) become dependent on care and require constant support.

Compared to the 1950s, the emancipation of women from the traditional roles of housewife and mother has strengthened the trend by both genders of defining (marital) partnerships as personally fulfilling, happy relationships. A new definition of the traditional role of women and their assimilation of what have up until now been typical male behavioural patterns has been gradually observed since the 1980s

This development already begins in adolescence. Girls' performances are now clearly superior to boys – especially in the development task of 'qualifying'. This development continues into adulthood, because more and more women are turning their backs on such limited tasks as housekeeping, raising children and committing to social engagement and instead are concentrating on a fourth area, namely their careers. Their educational achievement is certainly of benefit here. This development is reflected in the female employment rate, which has steadily increased over the last 30 years. This trend was minimally affected by economic developments and continued unabated even during economic crises. The percentage of employed males steadily decreased during the same time frame. These trends also symbolically convey the strong urge women have to fundamentally change their social role in modern society and to take an active part in economics and, increasingly, in politics.

However, there are large subgroups of women and men independent of this development who do not completely fulfil the traditional social status of adult because they are not employed and do not live in a family context with own children. If we apply the criteria of the accomplishment of developmental tasks specific for this age, these groups have avoided two decisive task areas (employed professional and family founder), but the public perceives them less and less often this way. When adults consciously decide not to have children, it is no longer perceived as a rebellion against predefined role expectations, which also applies to unemployment under certain circumstances (e.g. in the case of disability or intensive care work). In this way, and contrary to the original idea of the developmental tasks concept, more and more areas are emerging which allow for an expanded definition of 'successful' accomplishment.

- **Developmental task consumption:** As in adolescence, an extremely high variety of offers by the media and leisure world is available and as adults they usually have the required financial resources to use them. Just as in adolescence, the mainly commercially controlled media offerings require a well-structured concept of how to use them.

- **Developmental task participation:** Similar to adolescents, adults require a sensitive grasp of the difficulties of future planning, especially in regard to such risks as unemployment, environmental pollution, health hazards and threat of war. Just as adolescents, adults will only be able to cope with their developmental tasks if they are convinced of their self-efficacy.

Coping with developmental tasks in the life stage senior

The transition from adulthood to old age – which shall be referred to as 'seniorhood' here – flows just as smoothly today as the transition from adolescence to adulthood. During the era of the standard biography in the twentieth century, the transition to seniorhood for employed men took place almost automatically on the day of retirement. The majority of unemployed women were also significantly affected by their (marital) partners' retirement, which proved to be a dramatic step in that it changed the entire course of domestic and leisure activities, as well as the maintenance of social contacts (Bengtson and Settersten, 2016).

Today, these transitions are much more diverse. This largely has to do with increased longevity. In early seniorhood, between the ages of 60 and 75, the physiological capacity decreases when compared with adulthood and the risk of chronic illnesses increases. However, the 'young senior' group as a whole is in good or at least satisfactory mental and physical health and for the most part is not dependent on help or care. On average, the material resources available are also good. This makes it possible to continue leading a lifestyle similar to the lifestyle led during adulthood, which also includes engaging in (part-time) professional activities. Therefore, for part of the population the first phase of seniorhood is almost indistinguishable from the previous adult life. This changes in the second phase of seniorhood beyond the age of 75, when physical and mental strengths decrease significantly.

What are the typical challenges today in coping with the developmental tasks of the life stage of seniorhood?

- **Developmental task qualifying:** Today, in most European countries withdrawal from active working life at around age 65 marks the transition to retirement for approximately half of the adult population, including an increasing number of women. This event is of no great importance for the remainder of the elderly population; some had already withdrawn from professional activity at the end of traditional adulthood due to health reasons or labour market conditions (early retirement), others continue to pursue part-time professional activities past the age of 65.

  No matter when retirement takes place – leaving a professional career means sociologically the loss of a distinct role that must be individually processed, and makes a new concept for the future necessary. Leaving the social framework of employment is often a relief from difficult conditions and stressful demands linked to the work process, but at the same time a person loses the feeling of recognition that makes him or her feel productive, useful and valuable to society.

People who withdraw from active working life are also faced with the task of mentally detaching themselves and finding new, publicly recognised forms of social activity (such as engagement in the social sector). The most successful people to assimilate to this stage of life seem to be those who maintain their private activities after retirement and tailor them to their individual level of activity. It is helpful to remember that a broad range of social roles within the family, neighbourhood and community are available, and that commitment in one of these roles can help balance and compensate for retirement. An alternative offers the numerous possibilities of finding new professional employment.

- **Developmental task bonding:** The living conditions of today's seniors hardly differ from those of adults in the area of partnership and relationships. The majority of seniors no longer have children living at home; they are free to shape their own relationships with friends and acquaintances and at the same time maintain the relationship to their children's families, including possible grandchildren. In old age, many partners have already died and new partnerships are often formed. Approximately one-third of seniors have formed a new partnership after their first marriage or relationship, which often includes children. This results in a diverse network of partnerships, friendships and family relations.

Increased longevity also results in diversified generational relationships. As grandparents or even great-grandparents, they are experiencing their grandchildren or even great-grandchildren more often. Thus, their network of relationships can include up to four generations of relatives living at the same time.

- **Developmental task consumption:** On the whole, the physical, psychological and social life situation of old people has steadily improved. Today's 70-year-olds demonstrate a level of health and performance found in 60-year-olds living 30 years ago. The good economic situation also has a positive effect on shaping leisure and consumer activities, including travel and social engagement.

The risk of health failure and functional decline grows only in late seniorhood, after the age of 75, and forces the restriction of many activities. The need for help and care on average grows during this life stage. The loss of social contacts increases through the deaths of friends and acquaintances. As the social networks within and outside of the family become successively smaller, feelings of isolation and loneliness may also set in.

The ageing process is a complex interaction between physical and psychological characteristics and the conditions of the spatial, social and institutional environment. The loss of the organism's vital capacity is expressed by the difficulties of the body's individual organs and functional systems to adapt and compensate, and is part of the normal biological and physiological process of ageing. The organs are no longer as resistant in seniorhood and do not have sufficient functional reserve. Blood pressure and blood lipid levels increase, the muscle fibres and vessels become weaker, the skeleton loses stability, eye lenses become blurred and hearing decreases. This natural, physical ageing process can be slowed by an active lifestyle (sport, movement, social activities and public engagement) but cannot be avoided.

Compared to men, women seem able to significantly delay the ageing process in the life course. They have greater immunological potential and live healthier than men overall. They employ preventive strategies more often (such as a healthy diet, a fixed daily rhythm, and effective relaxation to avoid the consequences and side-effects of chronic physical illnesses) in order to keep up with daily activities and strengthen the existing health potential. Through this, they promote their physical and psychological function and have a significantly higher life expectancy.

- **Developmental task participation:** This results in various individual potentials for social engagement and political participation in seniorhood, whose scope can range from the conventional 'retirement' of a 65-year-old teacher following two heart attacks to the full-time activities of a 75-year-old businesswoman.

Questions

1   Which problems can occur today in coping with the developmental tasks of the life stage childhood?

2   Which problems can occur today in coping with the developmental tasks of the life stage adolescence?

3   Which problems can occur today in coping with the developmental tasks of the life stage adulthood?

4   Which problems can occur today in coping with the developmental tasks of the life stage senior?

Answers

1   Childhood today means to be a 'digital native' permanently exposed to information, living in insecure social relationships and in a competitive society in which only individual performance counts. Childhood also means to live in a world with high performance expectations of parents, educators and teachers, with a leisure market that is characterised by consumption and commercial stimuli, to experience the increasing shortage of play areas and open spaces in the living environment. Finally, childhood also means the experience of hardly having the chance to actively influence these processes.

2   The high performance expectations that already exist in childhood further increase and are experienced as strong pressure by many adolescents. Today, high-level education and training qualifications have become necessary but by no means sufficient prerequisites for acceptance in the professional world during times of job shortages and international competition. When it comes to bonding, tensions and mood swings must be experienced to the full extent to develop a mature personality structure, and the ability to balance the requirements of individuation and identity and establish an efficient self-identity. The mainly commercially controlled media offerings require a well-structured concept of how to use them; otherwise, they can lead to ecstatic consumption patterns and a danger of addiction. Despite all these worries and concerns, they will only be able to cope with their developmental tasks if they are convinced of their self-efficacy, or in other words, are confident enough to master the requirements of their life despite all the adverse circumstances.

3   The life stage of adulthood is traditionally defined by assuming the role of breadwinner and founding a family. As a result of the extended life stage of adolescence, both of these social milestones are now occurring at very different points in time. As such, the onset of the life stage adulthood is occurring much later in life. Adulthood has not remained unaffected by the precarious economic conditions of the last few decades. Interrupted or even abandoned careers during periods of mass unemployment prove to be challenging for biography management in the life stage mature adulthood. Compared to the 1950s, the emancipation of women from the traditional roles of housewife and mother has strengthened the trend by both genders of defining (marital) partnerships as personally fulfilling, happy relationships. A new definition of the traditional role of women and their assimilation of what have up until now been typical male behavioural patterns has been gradually observed since the 1980s.

4.   No matter when retirement takes place – leaving a professional career means the loss of a distinct role that must be individually processed, and makes a new concept for the future necessary. Leaving the social framework of employment is often a relief from difficult conditions and stressful demands linked to the work process, but at the same time a person loses the feeling of recognition that makes him or her feel productive, useful and valuable to society. Many partners have already died and new partnerships are often formed. This results in a diverse network of partnerships, friendships and family relations. The risk of health failure and functional decline grows in late seniorhood, after the age of 75, and forces the restriction of many activities. The need for help and care grows during this life stage. The

loss of social contacts increases through the deaths of friends and acquaintances. As the social networks within and outside of the family become successively smaller, feelings of isolation and loneliness may also set in.

Contexts of socialisation in the life course

6

The previous chapters clearly demonstrate how great the challenges are for the effective processing of the internal and external reality in the individual phases of the life course. In Chapter 1 we identified the most important achievement of socialisation theory as the ability to answer two related questions:

- How does a society manage to shape the human beings living in this society into social beings who integrate themselves into the existing social structures?

- How do human beings manage to open up opportunities for their own personal development and lifestyle and become autonomous individuals in a society?

Chapters 3, 4 and 5 have shown that the highly developed western societies grant their citizens great freedoms for personal development and lifestyle, and make only vague overtures to integrate into the social structures. In each phase, developmental tasks are confronted which must be understood by every person, translated into own possibilities, transformed into action and finally scrutinised according to own standards.

As the previous chapters show, external control through social norms and regulations is not sharply contoured, so that a significant degree of freedom remains for personal structuring. For the most part, developmental tasks are not defined in detail by society; very often it is only the goals that are formulated, such as 'take on a professional role' or 'deal with the media confidently', but the way of achieving these goals is left up to the individual. This raises the question of which role the structures and contexts of socialisation play in modern European societies.

The significance of socialisation agents

Socialisation always takes place in a social context. Personality development requires long-term support in processing the internal and external reality. Supporting contexts, institutions and settings can be designated as 'socialisation agents' or also as 'socialisation contexts'. The most prominent contexts are the family and the educational systems.

Family

The family serves as the primary and most important social-isation context in our culture. For centuries it has acted as the most influential agent of external reality for each successive generation. It is often designated as the 'primary socialisation agent' because for most people it is the first and most important social environment. Beginning in early childhood, social, cultural and economic living conditions are reflected in a family which impact personality development, as in a microcosm (Flanagan, 1999).

Generally formulated, a family is characterised by long-term cohabitation with relatives from several generations, who as a rule are related and connected by caregiving or educational relationships. The concrete social form the family takes is largely dependent on the economic and cultural framework of a society. A very pronounced change has taken place in this respect within the last 100 years. In view of the rapidly changing familial involvement, the highly interesting question arises of whether families – despite their diminishing temporal influence on the personality development of their members – still retain their formative significance for the personality.

It is also interesting to know which forms of cooperation between families and organised educational institutions lead to optimal results in personality development. The underlying question is which individual competences a personality in the modern world must possess in order to deal with the diversity of socio-spatial contexts and influences, and to promote healthy physical and psychological development. The main questions regarding this issue are those which refer to the minimum competences required by a person to participate and integrate in a modern society. So far, we have seen how much the social functions of the family have changed within the last 100 years. Families have become small and specialised social systems which, along with preserving the parents' relationship, merely serve to care for and support the children, albeit with strong limitations. Important social functions, such as work, house-keeping, social security provisions in illness and retirement, care and support have been removed from the family and outsourced to specialised systems.

Education system

The task of education has been removed from the family step by step and outsourced to specialised institutions. In this way, a differentiated education system from day care centres to primary school to university has been created, and since the era of industrialisation, and especially since the introduction of compulsory education in 1900, has continued to expand temporally and socially. A member of society spends the entire life stages of childhood and adolescence in the system, which, along with vocational training and professional development, also plays an increasingly important role in adulthood and seniorhood (Apple, Ball and Gandin 2010).

Secondary socialisation agents and contexts are gaining in importance, among them public education institutions such as nursery schools, day care centres, schools, training institutions, universities, social-pedagogic institutions and vocational institutions, which have been established explicitly for this purpose. While mothers and fathers serve as 'amateur educators' in the socialisation agent family, professional educators devoted to pedagogy work in the education system. Since educational institutions are 'secondary' agents, educators depend on the groundwork laid in the family home, which is the 'primary' agent. As the basic structures of children's personalities have already been shaped by this time, educators must integrate this groundwork and build upon it. There has been an increase in the self-organisation of education at all levels of the system, which can be attributed to the influence of digitalisation. Today, the typical learner is more than willing to take control of his or her learning performance. He or she has become a broker for his or her personal abilities and competences, and gears their lifestyle toward the achievement of educational success. As such, the learner virtually takes on the role of his or her own 'education manager'.

To meet this development, every member of society – beginning with kindergarten, through school and on up to professional training – is faced with the challenge of creating an individual educational biography. This has to do with lifelong learning, which ideally corresponds to the concept of socialisation as an active and productive processing of the internal and external reality during the entire lifespan. As has been discussed, the sociological as well as bio-medical and brain research emphasise the lifelong restructuring of abilities, action competences and structures of perception and reaction of human beings, which can be promoted by adequate favourable environmental impulses. Equally important for the optimal development of social and cognitive competences is an arrangement of stimulating learning impulses which provide intense guidance and instruction, but at the same time afford enough freedom for the further self-directed development of abilities and competences.

Socialisation in the everyday life world

In addition to families and education institutions as primary and secondary socialisation agents, there exist several social systems that were not explicitly established to influence the personality development of its members but which are nevertheless significantly relevant for socialisation. These are institutions of the everyday life world and serve as 'tertiary' socialisation agents.

Families are the primary socialisation agents because they shape the basic structure of a personality and support it in developing patterns for processing the internal and external reality. Public education institutions are secondary socialisation agents because they systematically convey social and performance competences important for the private and professional life, and achieve this by building upon the socialisation and educational groundwork laid by the families.

The tertiary socialisation agents have long been ignored. They have become very important in today's complex and highly differentiated societies and are closely intertwined with the primary and secondary agents of socialisation. The gainful employment of parents for example, as well as the joint use of mass media in families have direct and indirect effects on and set the social context for socialisation. Therefore, socialisation influences can often not be distinguished from one another (e.g. Krijnen and van Bauwel, 2015).

In highly developed societies there exists a wide range of socialisation agents and systems whose essential functions lie not in socialisation, upbringing, education and qualification but rather in the fulfilment of other societal tasks. These include

- informal contexts such as intimate partnership, peers, friends and acquaintances, and

- formal contexts such as institutions and organisations for gainful employment and professional life, leisure and consumption, information and entertainment (media), practice of religion and value orientation and political institutions.

These social systems attract people over a longer period of time and integrate them into their structure. For this reason, they exercise a significant influence on the personality development of their members or users, although they were not normally established for this particular purpose.

In the following, we will investigate the most important social systems that influence the way reality is processed.

Partnership

Partnerships, the cohabitation of two people over a longer period of time, shape the personalities of both parties involved. Similar or even identical daily rhythms are a common result of living together. It is also common to see a homogenisation of taste and clothing, as well as of food and daily activity. It also leads to an intensive exchange of views and attitudes, and a convergence or even conformity in lifestyle and values, religious and political views and leisure and consumer habits. All of these influences have a great impact on personality development, since the partner relationship is based on eroticism and sex – irrespective if it is same-sex or mix-sexed (for a more complex perspective see Cover, 2016).

Partnerships can also be integrated into a family; as a rule, families are formed by the intimate cohabitation of two people in a love relationship. The partnership changes in character as soon as children are born but remains a relatively autonomous subsystem within the overall family system. During the periods prior to founding a family and after the children have moved out, this partnership is a social system which serves a lifestyle of two and does not fulfil any tasks in the area of upbringing or education. In all cases, the partnership is a socialisation-relevant system which strongly influences personality development.

Friends and peers

Beginning in childhood and adolescence, friends and peer groups bring people with similar needs and orientations together and fulfil their desire for community and participation. These groups accompany the process of detachment from the parents, complement the impulses stemming from school and prepare for the social demands of the leisure and consumer world (Schneider, 2016).

The exchange of views and feelings among people of equal rank and with comparable experiences is possible within a group of friends. The worries and problems of coping with developmental tasks are often dealt with. Friends seek understanding and solidarity, and support one another in forming their social life world. Trust also enables them to address topics dealing with emotions and sex that may not be approached within the family or partnership. Thus, friends are absolutely essential for their help and support.

The significance of friends for personality development has increased since virtual social networks such as Facebook were established around 2000. These networks make it possible to individually shape relationships and contacts in the most diverse forms and concentration, and in such a way that would be impossible in direct face-to-face exchange. Traditional social constraints are lifted by the global network, which opens communication opportunities that bridge spatial distances and overcome differences in social backgrounds, biological age and language.

This results in social contacts unforeseen in their scope and form that enrich personality development and provide numerous impulses for an expansion of the self-identity. The problematic side of this development is that many people feel under pressure to develop and maintain a broad and encompassing network of extremely diverse contacts that do not necessarily meet their own personal needs. Network users with inner insecurities and fragile self-identities can often be dragged into critical communication situations and commitments. This includes the marginalisation and degradation of those participating and aggressive insults and attacks (mobbing), initiation of business contacts in which the partner provides fake personal details with fraudulent intent and misuse of the network for erotic and sexual contacts. This clearly demonstrates the dangers that can result for the further personality development.

Occupational institutions

Gainful employment in occupational institutions, companies and firms secures the economic existence of an adult member of society and for this reason is incredibly important for the lifestyle. The character of the work, its temporal rhythm and its social integration influences many aspects of personality development. This is especially true now, when the availability of electronic information and communication media makes it so difficult to draw temporal and contextual boundaries between professional and personal life. In this way, employment can become the absolute dominant activity over longer periods of the life course and impact daily attitudes and actions that actually follow other social rules (Easterby-Smith and Lyles, 2011; Wanberg, 2012).

The socialisation effects of gainful employment in the professional sector can be identified on several levels, much as with organised education institutions: the direct, one-on-one relationship, the collective contact between the employees as a team, the relationships between supervisors and employees, and indirectly through the organisational structure. However, the focus on independent activities and the transformation to an employee-entrepreneur is becoming more and more important in light of insecure forms of employment and quickly changing job requirements. This can lead to an especially intense identification with the job and an apprehensive fixation with securing the professional existence, which influences personality development on an even greater scale.

Entering into a profession brings changes in action competences and self-definitions. In a company environment, new assessments of opportunities for further professional development and career perspectives are made under pressure to achieve good results, and the expectations developed during education and training must be adapted to the conditions at hand, which very often leads to painful adjustments. This can result in a grounding of high-flying career plans or alternatively, in an escalation of ambition and motivation. This career effect is not the only critical factor for occupational socialisation; also important are the structuring effects of the type of professional activity according to the degree of independence, the nature of the work and the position within a work hierarchy. The workplace climate, with its particular structuring of technical, organisational and communicative aspects, creates a social-isation environment that has a lasting effect throughout the individual's entire career; it is a central part of external reality, with much personal contact to colleagues and adjustment to values and life expectations.

Working conditions exercise a strong influence on the personality and life planning. The physical working conditions, the opportunities to make use of personal abilities, the rhythm of work activities and the variety of content, the speed and intensity of the workflow, the social conditions and interactive relationships, the prestige and the promotion opportunities, the method of payment and the entire income all prove to be decisive factors.

The introduction of modern information and commun-ication technology in daily work life has shifted professional requirements more and more in the direction of an individual-ised worker qualification profile, combined with the necessity of permanent adjustment to changed working conditions. This requires willingness to self-regulate personal performance.

Such a requirement profile demands professional flexi-bility and the pronounced ability to self-motivate, combined with a great sensitivity for imminent changes in the workflow. Employees become active brokers of their personal abilities and individual qualifications. Their own labour is permanently oriented to the economic benefit and specific needs of the company, and the personal assessment of benefits plays a significant role. Today's employee typically has much more temporal and spatial freedom and a much greater degree of autonomy in the organisation of his or her workflow than previously. However, due to the rigid self-discipline, the employee feels under extreme pressure to perform well and is forced to make self-organised work and learning the focus of life.

Leisure and consumer institutions

The confident use of consumer, media and leisure offerings is one of the central developmental tasks in every life stage. Because developmental tasks in the areas of 'qualifying' and 'bonding' are perceived as challenging and difficult, there is a great demand for entertainment, diversion and regeneration. Many different suppliers with increasing sophistication and an increasing amount of commercialisation provide these offers. This suggests that relaxation and fitness, leisure and pleasure can be 'bought' without having to actively work for it.

This approach goes hand in hand with cultivating an image and projecting a certain impression of the own personality and self-identity. This has led to an enormous increase in the importance of consumer goods for the development of the self-image. With the help of a certain product, people seek to gain access to a lifestyle or status they strive to achieve.

The manufacturers of consumer articles – from clothing to cars to home furnishings – take advantage of this and through design and advertising attempt to establish 'brand products' their customers can closely identify with. The brand products should be blatantly used as a type of 'second skin' to assume the identity of a person who possesses the desired lifestyle. In consumer-oriented societies, this mechanism of 'purchasing an identity' is especially attractive to people who have difficulty in developing a self-identity and who would like to divert themselves and the social environment from this problem.

Media

Mass media such as radio, television and internet allows informational participation in practically every area of life, but the use of interactive media (internet media) especially requires a high level of competence. The inexhaustible abundance of information requires the decoding, selection and evaluation of content for the own personal needs. The user must be able to recognise the messages contained within the texts and images as well as their significance, and to transfer this into their own realm of knowledge and experience. In searching for information, the user must be able to assess the relevance and credibility of content if he or she does not want to be run aground by biased, distorted or false statements from providers with commercial, political or religious intentions (in a broader sense see Lemish, 2013).

From a socialisation-theoretical perspective, usage according to personal needs is a decisive criterion in determining whether or not media exercises a positive influence on personality development, especially in mastering developmental tasks, combining individuation and integration and strengthening self-identity. Media competence will continue to grow as an important factor in a society's ability to act, since more and more often it is required for education and professional activities, and increasingly for consumer and political activities.

The media offers diverse reference points for self-staging and the definition of self-identity because it enables the production of own content. Personal artistic works, articles in electronic lexicons and contributions to products and services can be offered to a large range of random groups. The requirement for this kind of creative and spontaneous use is that the user possesses a broad mix of media knowledge, design and reflection. However, if a user is pushed into the passive role of consumer by the overwhelming abundance and dynamic of the medial forms and messages, this can lead to an 'instrumentalisation' of his or her needs and interests. The result can be disturbed, unbalanced personality and identity structures.

Religious and value systems

Socio-economic living conditions shape the value orientation and religious attitudes of people during the entire life course. In times of economic and political insecurity as today, materialistic values are experiencing a renaissance. The prevailing value orientation is a synthesis of 'old' materialistic and 'new' unmaterialistic orientations: diligence and ambition, power and influence as well as security as materialistic values are being combined with post-materialistic values of self-fulfilment, creativity, independence, enjoyment of life and quality of living. In view of the recent economic crisis during the years from 2005 to 2008, the majority of (mainly young) young people are aware that securing a material basis should be the focus of their lifestyle. Accordingly, they aim toward career advancement and are confident, at times selfish, in the realisation of their own interests. At the same time, they are willing to engage in social commitment (Killen and Smetana, 2007).

According to experience, after a while the value patterns of the young generation spread to the entire population. Consequently, there prevails a pragmatic and constructive standard of living that is characterised by a high performance motivation and ambition to resolutely seize the chance for personal development and preserve the own independence and freedom. At the same time, there dominates a great desire to secure a livelihood, protect environmental resources, belong to social networks and integrate in harmonious relationships. In this context, churches and religious communities are perceived by the majority of the population as offering set values, among other things. Those who do not draw on this are responsible for their own subjective model of the interpretation of life.

Religion plays a decreasing role for most people in most European societies. As a rule, the majority of the population belongs to one of the Christian or Orthodox churches, but only half of them are religious in the sense that they believe in a personal god (Collins-Mayo and Dandelion, 2010).

The minority assembles interpretations and value systems according to their own personal ideas or are nonreligious. However, the large majority of the population fundamentally accept churches and religious communities as a social authority of value setting who can provide support and guidance in times of important personal and biographical life steps and crises. But their concrete meaning for the shaping of daily life, the confrontation of daily conflicts, the coping with the developmental tasks at hand or the development of a self-identity is limited.

Political institutions

The huge majority of the European countries are democratic. Democracy is accepted as a state and social form, but the democratic practices implemented by today's political parties generate uneasiness, which leads to a wariness of the political system. This wariness increases when the personal life situation is considered unfavourable. This results in a decreasing trust that politicians and parties are capable of improving and compensating for the personal disadvantages (Percy-Smith and Thomas, 2009).

Thus, large segments of the population show a great deal of reserve towards the political apparatus. The parties are perceived as isolated systems that offer very few opportunities for personal co-determination. Many people are willing to assume responsibility in moderation and to fight for humanitarian goals and better living conditions, but they do not want to operate within the structures of a non-transparent political apparatus.

For these reasons, the willingness to engage politically and participate in the shaping and structuring of living conditions is restrained. The majority of the population participates in the community through their active involvement in the educational and professional area. For them, the individual mastering of problems in daily life is more important than working on the overall objectives of societal reform. Self-organisation of the own personality and biography management apparently require so much energy that there is little left to devote to political engagement.

However, as already mentioned, there is a fundamental willingness for social engagement, as well as for selective political activism. Because of dissatisfaction with the political processes of the parliamentary system, free associations and citizen initiatives benefit from this willingness, whereas the established parties have problems attracting enough membership.

Politicians are no longer considered a 'mouthpiece' for the interests and needs of the members of a society but rather as the functionaries of an elite cartel of party and government apparatuses. Many citizens feel they have no influence on the decisions made by the political cartels, which results in a dangerous mix of helplessness and alienation, combined with feelings of powerlessness and confusion. This is the main reason for the attractiveness of right wing populist parties in many European countries.

Questions

1   What are the dominant institutions designated as 'socialisation agents' or 'socialisation contexts'?

2   What are the main domains of socialisation in the everyday life world?

3   What are the specific socialisation effects of gainful employment?

4   What are the specific socialisation effects of the leisure and consumer sectors and the media?

5   What are the specific socialisation effects of value systems?

Answers

1   The family serves as the primary and most important socialisation context in our culture. For centuries it has acted as the most influential agent of external reality for each successive generation. It is often designated as the 'primary socialisation agent' because for most people it is the first and most important social environment. Secondary socialisation agents and contexts are gaining in importance, among them public education institutions such as nursery schools, day care centres, schools, training institutions, universities, social-pedagogic institutions and vocational institutions, which have been established explicitly for this purpose. While mothers and fathers serve as 'amateur educators' in the socialisation agent family, professional educators devoted to pedagogy work in the education system. Since educational institutions are 'secondary' agents, educators depend on the groundwork laid in the family home, which is the 'primary' agent.

2   In addition to families and education institutions as primary and secondary socialisation agents, social systems are gaining in importance that were not explicitly established to influence the personality development of its members but which are nevertheless significantly relevant for socialisation. These are institutions of the everyday life world and serve as tertiary socialisation agents. They have become very important in today's complex and highly differentiated societies and are closely intertwined with the primary and secondary agents of socialisation. These include institutions and organisations for work and professional life, practice of religion and value orientation, politics, media, entertainment, leisure time and regeneration, consumption, social contact and communication. These social systems

attract people over a longer period of time and integrate them into their structure. For this reason, they exercise a significant influence on the personality development of their members or users, although they were not normally established for this particular purpose. This is also the case for informal contexts such as intimate partnership, friends and acquaintances and the socio-ecological life world. These contexts, institutions and settings can be designated as 'tertiary' socialisation agents and contexts.

3   The introduction of modern information and communication technology in daily work life has shifted professional requirements more and more in the direction of an individualised worker qualification profile, combined with the necessity of permanent adjustment to changed working conditions. This requires willingness to self-regulate personal performance. Employees become active brokers of their personal abilities and individual qualifications. Their own labour is permanently oriented to the economic benefit and specific needs of the company, and the personal assessment of benefits plays a significant role. Today's employee typically has much more temporal and spatial freedom and a much greater degree of autonomy in the organisation of his or her workflow than previously. However, due to the rigid self-discipline, the employee feels under extreme pressure to perform well and is forced to make self-organised work and learning the focus of life.

4   The confident use of consumer, media and leisure offerings is one of the central developmental tasks in every life stage. Because developmental tasks in the areas of 'qualifying' and 'bonding' are perceived as challenging and difficult, there is a great demand for entertainment, diversion and regeneration. Many different suppliers with increasing

115

sophistication and an increasing amount of commercialisation provide these offers. This suggests that relaxation and fitness, leisure and pleasure can be 'bought' without having to actively work for it. This has led to an enormous increase in the importance of consumer goods for the development of the self-image. With the help of a certain product, people seek to gain access to a lifestyle or status they strive to achieve. The use of interactive media (internet media) especially requires a high level of competence. The inexhaustible abundance of information requires the decoding, selection and evaluation of content for the own personal needs. The user must be able to recognise the messages contained within the texts and images as well as their significance, and to transfer this into their own realm of knowledge and experience. In searching for information, the user must be able to assess the relevance and credibility of content if he or she does not want to be run aground by biased, distorted or false statements from providers with commercial, political or religious intentions.

5   Socio-economic living conditions shape the value orientation and political attitudes of people during the entire life course. In times of economic and political insecurity as today, materialistic values such as diligence and ambition, power and influence as well as security are experiencing a renaissance. These are being combined with such post-materialistic values of self-fulfilment as creativity, independence, enjoyment of life and standard of living. In view of the economic crisis, the majority of people are aware that securing a material basis should be the focus of their lifestyle. Accordingly, they aim toward career advancement and are confident, at times selfish, in the realisation of their own interests. At the same time, they are willing to engage in social commitment.

Inequality of socialisation during the life course

7

Highly developed societies are characterised by a large spectrum of economic, social and cultural inequality. This results in differences in the socialisation processes of segments of the population with a high and low socio-economic status. People who live in a privileged context have access from birth on to a more comprehensive range of personal and social resources in their everyday environment than those who live in a disadvantaged context. This leads to a lifelong unequal distribution of life opportunities (for a broader perspective see Brady and Burton, 2016).

Inequality is the result of contextual and compositional differentiation and can have serious disadvantages for life-styles that are difficult to resolve (Alexander, Entwisle and Olson, 2014). The illustrative example of the young man in the underground station in Chapter 1 refers to this differentiation. Just as a reminder: *Contextual* factors concern the material features, the symbolism and standardisation of a space in which people act. *Compositional* factors describe the composition of a group to which people belong or in which they act. Both dimensions determine the forms and profiles of inequality.

The imbalance between the social life situations has increased in almost all of the wealthy European countries within the last three decades. Social structure and inequality research emphasises the horizontal and vertical patterns of inequality but above all sees the highly developed European societies as testimony of an increasing social polarisation and considers the perspective of socialisation processes as the key to understanding the transfer of not only privileges but also of disadvantages from one generation to the next.

Inequality of socialisation in the individual life stages

Though we live in an individualistic society, economic and social framework conditions still determine the space for individual lifestyles and coping with developmental tasks. In contrast to the early discourse on inequality, multifaceted inequality is now at the core of current debate. While the understanding of inequality heavily leaned on the rhetoric of materialism right up into the 1970s, the discussion was broadened in the years following. It is now a matter of course that in the debate on inequality, not only are the classical forms of inequality distribution considered (assets, income and property) but also the significance of educational achievement (an aspect Bourdieu has described as cultural capital), social networks, mentality and lifestyle (Bourdieu, 1979/1984).

Earlier approaches of socialisation theory measured inequality one-dimensionally on a social rank from top to bottom. Traditional class-specific socialisation research maintained that economic resources were of sole relevance for the position of certain population groups within the hierarchy of social structure. The influences of cultural, social and ecological conditions were either ignored or insufficiently considered, as were those of subcultures with their contextual and compositional parameters, such as adolescent peer groups, family and sibling constellations, school, neighbourhood and residential environments and the influence of educational styles and potential.

In the meantime, the multidimensionality of socialisation areas, agents and effects has been thoroughly researched. Today, this focus on co-variants and the effects of interaction is associated with the influence of socio-ecological model concepts (Bronfenbrenner, 1979). A particular focus of socio-ecological research is the permanent and everyday (socialisation) contexts in which people interact without conscious awareness of such abstract influences as social class.

Inequality in childhood

The initial conditions for coping with developmental tasks differ greatly depending on the social background. The living conditions and educational impulses in the family home play a key role. Children who successfully face the complex challenges of the modern life world, and that is the large majority of them, have already developed the ability to realistically assess and implement their internal and external resources. They are usually supported by family homes that provide specific recognition and give them the encouragement and guidance they are able to process at each respective development stage. The better the economic situation, social integration and interconnectedness, and child-raising skills the parents have, the more favourable the conditions are for the children to have available the components needed today to successfully develop a personality with an independent lifestyle.

In comparison, children with less supportive family homes have much less margin for shaping their own lifestyle. Poverty and a lack of domestic resources lead to limited opportunities for participation: in the family, where material pressures and existential worries have already been registered by the children; at school, where the opportunity for individual support to compensate for existing disadvantages lacks; as well as in the residential environment, including the opportunity to participate in clubs. Children from the lower social classes are often left to rely on themselves. They lack encouragement, ideas and impulses, and targeted support. As a consequence, everyday life for a large number of these children consists mainly of television or other forms of media consumption.

Calderón-Almendros (2011) provides insight into the life world of deprived adolescents who perceive themselves as pushed aside and left behind, who live in poor districts, are without perspective and are opposed to the police and school because they stand for those who hold the power and influence. The interplay of perceived hopelessness and not taking advantage of the opportunities available becomes a vicious circle (especially when violence plays a role, Macmillan, 2001).

In contrast to this, children from the upper class are able to make use of their better opportunities right from the beginning, as they have a more suitable scope of margins. Their families' educational backgrounds provide them with access to a diverse and creative form of leisure and recreational activities. This is why they are able to develop the confidence to shape and create things themselves (self-efficacy). They employ more varied ways to build stable friendships and at the same time make the experience that their opinion is much more valued: Accordingly, these children have more faith and trust in their own core competence and learn to decide for themselves on how to approach and challenge their own lives in order to make use of the chances available to them. They are also confronted with risks in everyday life and feel a pressure to prove themselves. The difference, however, is that more paths are open to them, which makes them better able to develop the necessary confidence to face the diverse challenges of family, school, leisure time and friends.

Approximately one-fifth of the youngest population group in highly developed countries are in a relatively bad starting position, whereby the gap between the majority of the privileged and the minority of the disadvantaged has increased in the past several years. Thus, children have very unequal social pre-conditions available to master their developmental tasks and to develop the necessary competences already needed at their stage of life to engage in biography management.

Inequality in adolescence

This also applies in adolescence: The higher the socio-economic and educational status of the parents, the better an adolescent is able to develop the competences necessary to master developmental tasks. However, adolescents from families with a lower social status have unfavourable conditions for coping with and balancing individuation and integration. The chances of becoming a really competent planning agent for one's own life and in this sense, becoming the producer of one's own adolescent personality (doing adolescence), are therefore very unequally distributed.

Summarising the outcomes of youth and inequality studies show some wide disparities among adolescents. A large proportion of the young generation is able to utilise the opportunities resulting from today's conditions in a very productive manner and to their own advantage. They approach developmental tasks pragmatically and performance-oriented, and are able to solve them with skill and perseverance. These adolescents take complete advantage of the opportunities that result from their pioneer role in seeking out new social, cultural and technical trends. They devise innovative ways to shape and develop living conditions with fun and passion, and arrive at solutions that are often copied by older members of society because of their originality and practicality. For the most part, these adolescents come from family homes with well-educated parents who are in secure professional and economic positions. Parents pass this security on to their adolescent children just as they pass on the competence to master life's challenges with confidence. As such, the initial conditions for these adolescents are favourable, even in times of economic crisis or social upheaval.

Another large proportion of young women and men cope with the life stage adolescence well or satisfactorily, although this stage has changed greatly when compared with earlier eras. These adolescents deal with the existing conditions in a pragmatic and confident manner and try to use them to their optimal benefit. Their parents occupy the middle social position and must often make great efforts to master their personal and professional challenges but are always able to arrive at viable solutions. The adolescents in this group sense that it cannot be entirely ruled out that they fall into a precarious financial and professional situation in times of economic crisis or upheaval. They cover up these fears with a pragmatic and forward-looking attitude, even when their self-assurance suffers a bit of doubt now and again.

A minority of up to one fifth of young people is not sufficiently capable of coping with the high demands in the personal environment, in the educational and professional qualification, and in the use of leisure and media offers and opportunities. This minority has grown in the past decades. Some of these adolescents have significant difficulty in coping with developmental tasks typical of today. They live in a precarious situation and feel – justifiably – socially marginalised and left behind. Most of these disadvantaged adolescents come from relatively poor family homes and have a father or mother with very little education or none at all who are at stake of unemployment or who already are. A disproportionate number of them live in households that have already been dependent on state welfare benefits for a longer period of time. Many have had unfortunate or unhappy school careers, which is why some have left at the end without obtaining a certificate or degree.

Thus, the majority of adolescents today find themselves in a more or less satisfactory life situation; however, a minority is stuck in a marginal social position that can have a significant negative impact on their social and mental well-being, as well as their health. These adolescents are unable to withstand the pressure they are subjected to in today's society to prove themselves. Socially marginalised young people clearly feel that they are stuck in a precarious social life situation. They are at least subconsciously aware of the relatively high risk that they may be excluded permanently from the job market. Those left behind feel to some extent overrun by the complex social and economic circumstances of life and are not able to activate the high degree of biography management necessary for success in the education and professional system and for shaping their personal lives and leisure time. Their willingness for political engagement is also very limited.

Inequality in adulthood

For the large majority of the adult population, the opportunities to biographically shape the life course have steadily grown within the last 50 years. Due to the overall successful economic development and the stable political system in most of the European countries, the chances to shape adult life according to personal desires and goals have constantly increased. A wide range of social security systems has mitigated the risk of unemployment, even in the aftermath of the economic crisis from 2005 to 2008. This provided most adults with a larger scope for the subjective development of the personality.

This positive balance is also reflected in health and illness data. Compared to the 1950s and 1960s, the overall physical and mental level of health among the adult population has increased significantly, especially through improved hygiene, good housing opportunities, good nutrition and excellent medical and psychological care. This has led to a steady increase in life expectancy for both genders (Matud, 2017).

This does not apply or only with considerable limitation to a minority of the adult population. As is the case with children and adolescents, there is a gradually increasing minority of approximately 20 per cent who are currently disadvantaged and relatively poor. The economic and as a consequence also the social and cultural inequality increased during the 1990s and 2000s, fuelled in particular by high unemployment, which is reflected by the high number of welfare benefit recipients, for example. In many cases, the disadvantaged lifestyle has perpetuated itself, beginning in childhood, continuing into adolescence and on into adulthood. In this sense, adults also live in a four-fifths society that tends to exclude 20 per cent of its members based on its social and economic opportunity structure.

Inequality in seniorhood

The differences according to social background are also obvious in seniorhood and increase significantly in old age. This is particularly reflected in the balance of health. If an old person succeeds in strengthening his or her physical and social resilience to stabilise mental and physical functionality at a good level, then it is possible to preserve the cognitive performance, perception and memory capacity over a longer period of time. Seniors with a high level of education and in a good economic situation achieve the best results.

The basic lifestyle skills (personal hygiene, dressing, shopping and using transportation) diminish more quickly among socially disadvantaged seniors in old age than among the well off. The extent of social activities (visiting people, receiving visitors) and beneficial leisure activities (excursions, sport, social engagement, going to the theatre and cinema) differ according to social background. The socio-economic and educational levels also clearly determine in old age the amount of personal and social resources that can be used for mastering developmental tasks.

Changing characteristics of inequality

There is much debate in research on the dynamic social conditions of contextual and compositional inequality, which are very relevant for shaping life opportunities. The positions are sometimes highly contradictory. A historical glance shows that an awareness of social inequality had already increased during socialisation theory's founding phase at the end of the nineteenth and the beginning of the twentieth century, and that it would go on to become a significant issue (ISSC, IDS and UNESCO, 2016).

After the Second World War, the topic vacillated between opposing views of an increase and a decrease in inequality. Furthermore, the contours of an autonomous field of inequality research and social structure analysis have clearly developed within the last three decades from which, nonetheless (and paradoxically), the topic of inequality had threatened to disappear because sociological approaches wrongly assumed that the end of classical inequality distribution was near. Today, the most comprehensive theory seems to be one that can link the significance of unequal resources with the perspective of individual lifestyles.

A decisive step in expanding the perspective of inequality research is the realisation that inequality exists not only in a material form (as money and assets in the sense of economic capital) but also in an immaterial form. As already mentioned, Pierre Bourdieu (1979/1984) understands it in particular as cultural resource or cultural capital. Inequality of cultural capital is regularly identified today with unequal education capital, meaning the highest educational degree available, but this must be considered as a simplistic view of the subject.

Throughout history, the relative significance of economic, cultural and social capital has been subjected to steady transformation. Especially macrosocial conditions (such as the state of social equality, the qualification path leading to good positions, welfare state arrangements, economic initial conditions or the influence of social movements) can determine fluctuations in the spread of inequality structures. Inequality in the relevant areas of education, employment and health are traditionally the most thematised in academic discourse.

The increase of inequality

The concept of life opportunities is well suited for determining inequality. Opportunity structure has diverse points of reference:

- Various *degrees of access* to institutions that provide important commodities and resources (as a negative example, the institutional discrimination of low income groups in the area of education and health).

- Unequal strategies of the *purchase* and *acquisition* of commodities and resources that are considered relevant for inequality (as a negative example, the limited opportunity to acquire material wealth through work because of the necessity to use income to meet daily needs).

The differences in opportunity structure are currently increasing between families that are able to offer their children very good material living conditions, good nutrition, housing and clothing, an abundance of leisure and educational impulses and a good upbringing based on secure bonds, and families with deficits and weaknesses in all of these areas. These differences in social resources available to the primary socialisation agents are included in the productive processing of the external reality and have an effect on the development of children's personalities. From the beginning, children from socially privileged families have much better opportunities for coping with developmental tasks than children from socially disadvantaged families. The results by Lareau (2011) impressively demonstrate this, also in regard to health-related behaviour, self-efficacy or dealing with media and consumer offerings.

The accumulation of inequality

The differences in the initial conditions for personality development seldom balance out over the course of a lifetime. Instead, for the majority of children the path of development becomes permanent and reinforced. Secondary socialisation agents succeed in changing the course set in the family home for only a small number of children from disadvantaged families. This includes offsetting the deficits in performance and competence development (in the accumulation of social and cultural capital, as Bourdieu calls it), and thus in the development of identity.

As a rule, tertiary socialisation agents also strengthen exist-ing inequalities because – to mention only one example – leisure and media offerings are taken up according to the differ-ences in attitude, perception and ability already formed by the family and with them, the interrelated norms of behaviour. Thus, the 'social habitus' is so strongly developed that in a sense, it reproduces itself.

For the majority of children from privileged social groups, this leads to an accumulation of further privileges, for those from underprivileged social groups to further disadvantages in the process of reality processing. This is a productive process for children from both groups in the sense that it takes place actively, individually and in an exploratory way. The respective results of these processes – measured by the ability to combine individuation and integration and develop a self-identity – are extremely varied: the more privileged the initial conditions, the more successful the development of the personality.

Gender and ethnic diversity

The search for social inequality creates a greater sensitivity for further divisions and distinctions. They make the term diversity conceivable. Diversity is oriented on various lines of differentiation associated with physical features or impairments (age, gender and appearance) as attributed (and considered to be unchangeable) traits, as well as with group memberships and mentalities, which are descriptive and therefore considered as changeable (Skelton, Francis and Smulyan, 2013).

Gender diversity is of great significance for socialisation theory. It extends into practically every area of personality development. Men and women differ according to their sex chromosomes and sex hormones. To what extent these differences have a lasting influence on complex behaviour is still disputed in research. In a pure physiological respect, the result is a diverse construction of the sex organs, body and brain and hormonal balances. However, this physical dimension is heavily overlaid with cultural and educational influences. Stereotyped patterns dominate: The masculine lifestyle and with it the mastering of developmental tasks is described in our culture as activity-oriented. Men traditionally take on the role of a powerful and superior provider for themselves and members of their families. 'Typical male' behaviour includes overpowering competitors, establishing dominance, keen self-assertion, dissociation from others, expansion of the self and the conquest of social space. In this way, the own existence is secured and power is exercised.

This pattern is in contrast to the 'typical female' orientation, which can be described as community-oriented. In our culture, women traditionally play the role of housekeeper who tends to the social cohesion and functioning of the community. 'Typical female' behaviour includes an effort to be part of society and the desire to help shape it, an intense effort to cooperate and bond with others, as well as the development of relationships and networks. In this way, they also exercise their own form of power.

Gender diversity in the processing of reality

Societies arrange their members into different groups according to certain features. An especially permanent assignment is according to gender, which is a binary differentiation of men and women. The assumption of fixed features for those who belong to such a defined group is a social construction. This determines an area of expected behaviour and patterns for coping with developmental tasks. Femininity and masculinity are lived and individually constructed in that a man or a woman individually works with the inherent physiological characteristics, the physical constitution, the mental structures and capacities and the attributed expectations and matches them to the social and physical world ('doing gender'). Despite the margins for individual design, typical feminine and masculine patterns of the productive processing of reality prevail in everyday life.

It is almost impossible to differentiate what is inherent and what is due to environmental influence when considering the requirements that shape female and male roles. The enormous variability of 'typical' male and female behaviour (we must simply look at the revolution in gender roles within the past 50 years), however, indicates a much greater proportion of constructed behaviour that is stimulated and expected by the environment (including the primary, secondary and tertiary socialisation agents). The inherent genetic characteristics that determine the differences in physique and organs are reshaped by cultural ideas of masculinity and femininity. The difference between genders is to a significant extent determined by such social influences. Many gender-specific personality features and behaviours are obviously acquired and evolve during the socialisation process. Genetics and personality features serve as the starting position and space of opportunity for gender-specific development.

Gender-specific patterns in coping with developmental tasks

If we use the lifespan as an indicator for the successful coping of developmental tasks, women are in a much better position than men and have been for generations. Right at birth, female infants prove to be more resilient and robust than male infants and have a much lower mortality rate. These differences remain a lifetime and lead to an average of 6 more years of life. Social science studies have suggested within the last four decades that women especially make more of an effort than men during adolescence and young adulthood to actively adjust to the present demands in all life areas and to develop a flexible understanding of the female gender role. Young women strive to expand their scope of disposition and liberate themselves from their traditional positions in society.

The vivid picture of the life areas of kitchen, church and children illustrates this. These areas define the traditional segments of the female role and continue to be important orientation points for the majority of women. The majority of young women have flexibly developed these areas, defined them anew in their relation to one another and have also conquered one more, that of career. The lifestyle of women is thus oriented to a range of diverse and varied roles. This orientation seems to prepare women for the new life conditions of modern societies. The multiple orientations consequently lead to greater investment by women in their own education, since it is a basic requirement for entry into a professional career.

The starting position is different with young men. They do not yet see the advantage of a new interpretation of their genetic and culturally predisposed gender role. They are hesitant to add the traditional areas of kitchen, church and children to the traditional male role of career. The focus on career proved to be nothing but advantageous for their fathers and grandfathers, and led to powerful economic and social positions; the majority of young men would like to follow in their footsteps. The problem, however, is that career requirements have been massively restructured by the integration of new information and communication technology in everyday work, and that social living conditions are more openly structured than 30 years ago. This has eliminated firm standards of behaviour, so that the importance of social sensitivity, adapting to new conditions and establishing communication networks has increased. Traditional male strengths such as the battle for dominance and the forceful exercise of power have become obsolete. Teamwork, with a balance of interests and negotiating skills, has taken their place.

Flexible lifestyles of women

Young men who continue to rely on narrow traditional gender roles under these conditions unintentionally create a social prison for themselves that blocks their further development. This is clearly demonstrated by the empirically sound investigation carried out by Best and Bush (2016). According to this, a narrow, limited idea of gender roles and a sexist attitude in men with a low education level and the traditional role patterns of the parents including non-working mothers are correlated. Young men socialised in this way will be just as unable to satisfy the change in career demands as they will the growing integration of an instrumentally oriented professional life and an emotionally oriented personal life. They ignore the symbiosis of career and family that results from this.

In times of international competition and increased demands on performance in all career sectors, the ability to lead a flexible lifestyle and link various areas of life is a requirement for being and remaining active and productive (Hurrelmann and Quenzel, 2013). The willingness to invest in personal school success, the competence to engage in 'education management' for the own self, seems closely linked to this. Young women have steadily increased their educational performance at all levels in the last 30 years. Men, in contrast, have stagnated in their performance and count more often than not to the 'losers' in education.

Up until the late twentieth century, the typical masculine way of life management was the more dominant and as a result, men took over the leading roles in the key life areas of politics, economy and culture. Through domination and homogamy effects (the privilege of the own gender), they have also been able to retain these positions of power. Within the past four or five decades, however, a reversal seems to have been initiated. In highly developed societies, girls and young women currently have better initial conditions for the mastering of developmental tasks typical of adolescence. This results in a shift of the gender-specific inequality patterns in favour of women. Overall, young women stand out through a more flexible coping behaviour adapted to changing social conditions and are beginning to conquer areas of life traditionally dominated by men, such as professional education establishments and universities, and slowly, positions in the economy, politics and culture.

Breaking down gender-specific inequality

To balance the differences between young men and young women in coping with developmental tasks, gender-specific interventions should be introduced into the process of social-isation. The current issue is to support young women in transitioning to a career and to offer them help in combining professional and family obligations. Structurally, this support should be supplemented by flexible work time and a comprehensive offer of preschool and day care facilities for children. For young men, it is crucial that their deficits in school performance are balanced out. It is also essential to prepare them for a flexible understanding of the male gender role with the aim that they become just as able as young women to reconcile career and family activities.

Based on these considerations, targeted programmes for the advancement of boys should draw especially on the developmental task 'qualifying'. These approaches could be coupled with impulses to expand the one-sided orientation on the traditional male model and to develop a coordinated understanding of masculinity based on personal interests and abilities.

As we have shown, open and pluralistic modern societies place great demands on flexible biography management. What is required is the willingness and competence to take new paths, to cope with structural uncertainty and overcome it with self-discipline. This mix of using targeted resources through in-depth knowledge of personal potential and exhausting new opportunities of behaviour and development is difficult for the majority of young men. Apparently, they often lack the encouragement and impulses from the socialisation agents of family, kindergarten and school, and the environments relevant for socialisation, such as peer groups, friends and the media. In contrast, young women receive a variety of stimuli to openly and flexibly define their gender role, to be oriented to success in the career and on the labour market and through this, to break into traditional male areas. This has positive effects on their intellectual and school performance. The challenge is to also offer young men such stimulation.

Ethnic diversity and socialisation

The term diversity is widely used to describe gender differences in socialisation theory. Apart from that, it can also be used to describe ethnical differences. Ethnical differences are becoming ever more visible due to the high rate of immigration and emigration between countries with different cultures. Such 'migration-related' differences in lifestyle cut across all other differences; they add to the existing differentiations according to socio-economic status, education, gender, age and religion. Economic, social, biological and ethnical inequalities correspond to one another. These structures of social inequality (also termed intersectionality) can reinforce or neutralise each other depending on the composition of characteristics, on a ratio of components, which makes the difference (Quintana and McKown, 2008).

Forms of ethnic stigmatisation are of particular importance in the current discussion, when it comes to group-related inequalities and disadvantages. This is indicated by the results of various surveys discussed at the international level and elaborated very well with regard to access barriers and discrimination patterns in the area of education and health.

However, it must be reviewed in detail to what extent such differences associated with ethnical inequalities (e.g. discrimination in the educational sector) constitute an independent ethnical factor that can be considered as the real 'power factor'. Detailed studies show that in most cases, the economic and social profile of a group still seems to be most important in this context (for an impact perspective on perceived racism see Priest *et al.*, 2013). Thus, social status and the availability of resources seem to be the driving forces of these types of discrimination, rather than the ethnic background.

Actually, many examples indicate that poor school performance and migration status are only superficially related. If pupils with a migrant background are compared with their peers who have non-migrant backgrounds but the same social profiles (e.g. parents with the same level of education and professional training), the pupils with migrant backgrounds no longer stand out. Their 'ethnical background' is no longer important. The same applies vice versa. The children of well educated parents normally also belong to an educational elite, and their ethnic or migrant background is effectively no longer important.

The problematisation of ethnic diversity

Such examples for the non-applicability of the significance of ethnical background can be observed quite frequently. But this understanding is not yet part of the public perception. There is still a strong tendency to attribute differences in competences, performance or mentality to established group characteristics.

This is evidenced by many examples of everyday life. When a young student whose parents are from Italy gets a little loud, this is attributed to his 'passionate temperament'. This perception will accompany him over a longer period, and he will not be able to neutralise this label as easily as it was attributed to his person. However, the findings resulting from a socialisation theory perspective show an exact countertendency. Mentality patterns of ethnic groups are enormously variable. Adaptation to altered cultural spaces (i.e. contexts) takes place within a very short period, and the social profiles (economic, cultural and social capital) are much more important for the form of a specific mentality than assumed homogenous (i.e. established and inflexible) group characteristics.

These findings necessarily lead to the discussion of what is termed ethnical diversity. Actually, the label ethnicity/ migration includes a much greater number of differentiations and differences. Contextual and compositional effects of the spatial environment seem to function as moderators for access opportunities, as for example central goods in the education and health sector. A survey of Kirby and Kaneda (2006) shows: If individual characteristics are controlled (i.e. if personal compe-tences are equal), socio-ecological factors exert an independent influence on access opportunities to basic supplies, such as in the area of health care, for example. This results in conclusions on the chain of effects of social discrimination: Individual characteristics (income, level of education) should always be considered in conjunction with compositional and contextual effects. On this basis, the characteristics of stigmatisation (membership of particular groups) are emphasised which, just like infrastructural factors, can be relevant for the form of inequality or access barriers (distance to physician, etc.).

Dealing with inequality and diversity

A high degree of social inequality and diversity leading to discrimination constitutes a risk for the cohesion of a society. A gap between poor and rich population groups is perceived as just as unfair as the division between a powerful and a power-less gender and undermines the solidarity in a community.

Therefore, all highly developed societies should be interested in reducing social inequalities to a minimum level. In addition to structural socio-political interventions, interventions in the process of socialisation are particularly suitable because they can influence the competences of society members for coping with developmental tasks. The earlier supporting and balancing interventions take place in the life course, the greater the chance to overcome unequal starting positions for the personality development.

When we talk about heterogeneity, inequality, or diversity it also always means to think about well targeted and non-discriminating supporting policies designed to precisely address the existing demand structures. The supporting measures for parents aimed at facilitating the reconciliation of work and family life can serve as a small specific example in this context. When mothers and fathers enter gainful employment, they are able to assume another active role in the society apart from child education that allows them to provide for themselves and their families. International comparison shows that securing the gainful employment of parents proves to be a particularly helpful strategy in stemming socio-economic inequalities, which can be observed very clearly in the Scandinavian countries.

A large segment of the population groups with migrant backgrounds need targeted individual support. The integration of their adult members into the workforce, and support for the parents of these families in child education and care in close cooperation with pre-school establishments and schools, are the most effective strategies of social integration. Since modern societies depend on the immigration of young people from other countries because of their demographic development, they must give policies in this area highest priority.

When economic and social inequality in a society decrease, social cohesion and the willingness of the members to support each other and show solidarity increase. In the long-term, this also leads to a decrease in the level of conflicts and tension. A high degree of social cohesion in a community leads to a higher degree of shared and recognised values, a consistent interpretation of the social conditions, and a sense of responsibility for the community together with the willingness to get involved in public affairs. This not only strengthens the personality of each individual member of the society but, at the societal level, also increases the collective power of innovation and production because people perceive themselves as members of a community. Socialisation plays a key role in this process, and therefore interventions in the socialisation process, as discussed above, are of great importance.

Questions

1   What is the main reason for the unequal distribution of life opportunities?

2   What are the reasons why in almost every European country about 20 per cent of the young people are stuck in a precarious and marginalised social position?

3   What is the reason for the preservation of inequality from one generation to the next?

4   Why do young women currently have better initial conditions for the mastering of developmental tasks?

5   What are the main effects of ethnic diversity on socialisation?

6   What is the role of socialisation theory in reducing social inequalities?

Answers

1   Economic, social and cultural inequality results in differences in the socialisation processes of segments of the
population with a high and low socio-economic status.
People who live in a privileged context have access from
birth on to a more comprehensive range of personal and
social resources in their everyday environment than those
who live in a disadvantaged context. This leads to a lifelong
unequal distribution of social opportunities.

2   Most of the disadvantaged children and adolescents come
from relatively poor family homes and have a father or
mother with very little education or none at all who are at
stake of or are already in unemployment. A disproportionate
number of them live in households that have already been
dependent on state welfare benefits for a longer period of
time. Many have had unfortunate or unhappy school
careers, which is why some have left the educational system
without obtaining a certificate or degree. As socially
marginalised young people they are aware of the relatively
high risk that they may be excluded permanently from
the job market. They feel to some extent overrun by the
complex social and economic circumstances of life and
are not able to activate the high degree of biography
management necessary for success in the education and
professional system, and for shaping their personal lives and
leisure time. Their willingness for political engagement is
also very limited because they do not have a feeling of self-
effectiveness.

3   Secondary socialisation agents such as kindergarten and
school as a rule do not succeed in changing the course set
in the primary socialisation in the family home. Therefore,

the deficits in performance and competence development continue during childhood and adolescence. In a similar vein, tertiary socialisation agents also strengthen existing inequalities. For the majority of children from privileged social groups, this leads to an accumulation of further privileges, for those from underprivileged social groups to further disadvantages in the process of reality processing.

4   Up until the late twentieth century, the typical masculine way of life management was the more dominant and as a result, men took over the leading roles in the key life areas of politics, economy and culture. Within the past four decades, however, a reversal seems to have been initiated. Young women stand out through a more flexible coping behaviour that is effectively adapted to changing social conditions. They are beginning to conquer areas of life traditionally dominated by men, such as professional education establishments and universities, and slowly, positions in the economy, politics and culture.

5   Ethnical differences are becoming ever more visible due to the high rate of immigration and emigration between countries with different cultures. Such 'migration-related' differences in lifestyle cut across all other differences: They add to the existing differentiations according to socio-economic status, education, gender, age and religion. Economic, social, biological and ethnical inequalities correspond to one another. These new patters of intersectional social inequality influence the personality development of migrants. This compounds the process of coping with developmental tasks and creating a self-identity.

6   Socialisation theory supports bi-directional strategies: structural socio-political interventions to decrease economic

and social inequality in a society ('external reality'), combined with interventions in the process of building competences of individuals ('internal reality') for coping with developmental tasks. A low level of social inequality in a society leads to a higher degree of shared and recognised values, a consistent interpretation of the social conditions, and a sense of responsibility for the community together with the willingness to get involved in public affairs. This in turn strengthens the personality of each individual member of the society and allows for the development of self-efficacy and self-identity.

Conclusion and outlook

Our book started accessing socialisation as a theoretical perspective. The argumentation included a bird's eye rather than a compartmentalised perspective. It stated that socialisation is an academic term used in research to describe the personality development of human beings in permanent interaction with their physical and psychological disposition on the one hand and the social and ecological living conditions on the other. The general framework refers to an individual perspective of dispositions, competencies and personality features (Grusec and Hastings, 2016). This implies a constantly mediating process between structure and agency in a life-course perspective.

Interestingly enough, there is an amazing amount of concepts deriving from educational, psychological and sociological research, as well as from health sciences, biographic research or research into aging applying the term of socialisation. Although we highlighted the active part of each individual within socialisation practices (the permanent confrontation with internal and external requirements), the real substance of socialisation is the integration of social values and norms. The so-called 'adaptation to social environments' is still a core concept within socialisation research. And there still is an essential spill-over into key issues of research on social integration or social (in)equalities. All of these theories need a perspective on socialisation that highlights the impact of social contexts and different environments on the capabilities of everyone's development.

The meta-theoretical model that has been applied in this book to analyse the life course dynamics is an ideal starting point for all of these approaches. The model of *Productive Processing of Reality* (*PPR*) places the human subject as dependent from a social and ecological context that is at the same time always influenced, changed and shaped by the subject itself. Personality development in this sense results from the productive processing of internal and external realities of the subject. The physical and mental dispositions and characteristics constitute the 'internal' reality, the conditions of the social and physical environment the 'external' reality.

As has been shown in Chapter 1 and 2, it took a long time to overcome a deterministic perspective on personal development that dominated the socialisation paradigm within the social sciences for decades. As a new framework, we postulate a lifelong active process by a human being of acquiring and processing natural dispositions and social and physical environmental conditions. Necessarily, limitations of each individual capacity have to be taken into account in order to avoid a perspective that neglects the structuring effect of living conditions. These conditions still differ widely concerning physical and social environments. Thus, structures of personality development are neither independent from social structures nor determined by them. Instead, the personality unfolds in the interplay between the individual, its developing competences and variables concerning diverse environments of each individual. The analysis of the human life course in modern societies is therefore first and foremost empirically oriented. A theoretical perspective can only open up a certain framework of research. Basic issues concerning social mobility, the importance of social support or, vice versa, discrimination and disadvantages can only be identified through research that is sensitive for both, the social and the individual side of capabilities.

Forthcoming activities in socialisation research will certainly highlight issues that are associated with questions of social justice and equal opportunities of the individual. Furthermore, changing life course regimes due to changing demands of workplaces will play an important role in upcoming research. What will be the consequences for biographical self-management, if manual work will fully disappear in developed countries whereas opportunities and necessities of a lifelong learning will overwhelm our lifestyles even more than today? How will education systems as institutions of secondary socialisation change? What does it mean if production work will take place in the periphery of the globalised world? What happens if refugee flows change the ethnic compositions of the populations of the welfare states of the West?

Socialisation theory will certainly be among the scientific approaches that will demand attention in the analysis of the society of tomorrow. We are deeply convinced that the interplay between psychology, sociology and neurosciences will be most important for future socialisation research. Great paradigm shifts took place already. The panorama – from a determination through social structures to an individual as a productive processor of internal and external reality and thus as a producer of the own development – cannot be widened anymore. Innovations may, as we have mentioned in Chapters 2 and 3, be expected by the neurosciences and particularly by epigenetics. Increasing knowledge about the epigenetic structure that is influenced by the environment will help to lighten up the black box of person-environment-interactions leaving their marks in basic human dispositions. Interestingly, the neurobiological approaches serve foremost as advocates of a new wave of environment-oriented research within the socialisation framework. They show how 'deep' experiences with social interactions reach inside a person's general physical and cognitive equipment.

The model of *Productive Processing of Reality* encourages interdisciplinary approaches from different theoretical perspectives. It will be helpful in future research to grasp the different structures of a person's integration into different environments (symbolic, social and material) during the life course and to understand the overlapping character of today's integration practices within different system levels. It can be applied to analyse the problems of identity formation in the twenty-first century with the peculiar mixture of experience and knowledge, which have to build upon each other in order to lead to a cohesive perception of the own personality and a coherent scheme of cognitive and behavioural orientation. Future socialisation research has to meet the challenge to offer new concepts that are sensitive enough to encompass attitudes, competencies and other identity 'features'.

Basic and applied knowledge production remains the focus of efforts in the field of socialisation research. Basic research will contribute to extended insights into the mechanisms of human development, social integration and social stability. Applied research will contribute to a set of strategies that promote the availability of best possible living conditions for each member of society with a specific focus on those members who live under disadvantaged conditions.

Bibliography

Alexander, K., Entwisle, D. and Olson, L. (2014) *The long shadow: Family background, disadvantaged urban youth, and the transition to adulthood*, New York: Russell Sage Foundation.

Anderson, V. and Beauchamp, M. H. (eds) (2012) *Developmental social neuroscience and childhood brain insult: Theory and practice*, New York: Guilford Press.

Antonovsky, A. (1979) *Health, stress, and coping* (1st edn), San Francisco: Jossey-Bass Publishers.

Apple, M. W., Ball, S. J. and Gandin, L. A. (eds), (2010) *The Routledge international handbook of the sociology of education*, London, NY: Routledge.

Archer, M. S. (2012) *The reflexive imperative in late modernity*, Cambridge, NY: Cambridge University Press.

Arnett, J. J. (2014) *Adolescence and emerging adulthood: A cultural approach* (4th edn), New York: Pearson Education.

Bandura, A. (1977) *Social learning theory*, Oxford: Prentice-Hall.

Bauer, U. (2013) *Sozialisation und Ungleichheit: Eine Hinführung (2. überarbeitete Auflage)* [Socialisation and inequality: An introduction (2nd rev. edn)], Wiesbaden: VS Verlag für Sozialwissenschaften.

Beardslee, W. R. (2009) *Out of the darkened room: When a parent is depressed: Protecting the children and strengthening the family*, New York: Hachette Book Group.

Beck, U. (1992) *Risk society: Towards a new modernity*, New Delhi: Sage.

Bengtson, V. L. and Settersten, R. A. (eds) (2016) *Handbook of theories of aging* (3rd edn), New York: Springer Publishing Company.

Berger, P. L. and Luckmann, T. (1966) *The social construction of reality: A treatise in the sociology of knowledge*, New York: Penguin Books.

Best, D. L. and Bush, C. D. (2016), 'Gender roles in childhood and adolescence', in U. P. Gielen and J. L. Roopnarine (eds), *Childhood and adolescence: Cross-cultural perspectives and applications*, California: ABC-CLIO, pp. 199–229.

Blakemore, S.-J. (2008) 'The social brain in adolescence', *Nature Reviews Neuroscience, 9*(4), 267–277. doi:10.1038/nrn2353.

Bourdieu, P. (1984). *Distinction: A social critique of the judgement of taste* (R. Nice, Trans.), London, NY: Routledge, Taylor & Francis Group (Original work published 1979).

Bourdieu, P. (1990) *The logic of practice* (R. Nice, Trans.), Stanford: Stanford University Press (Original work published 1980).

Brady, D. and Burton, L. M. (eds), (2016) *The Oxford handbook of the social science of poverty*, New York: Oxford University Press.

Bronfenbrenner, U. (1979) *Ecology of human development: Experiments by nature and design*, Cambridge: Harvard University Press.

Bruer, J. T. (1999) *The myth of the first three years: A new understanding of early brain development and lifelong learning*, New York: Free Press.

Bühler-Niederberger, D. (2016) 'Childhood socialization', in G. Ritzer (ed), *Wiley Blackwell encyclopedia of sociology* (2nd edn), New York: Wiley, pp. 344–354.

Calderón-Almendros, I. (2011) 'Breaking away to find a way: poverty and school failure in a Spanish adolescent life-history', *British Journal of Sociology of Education, 32*(5): 745–762. http://dx.doi.org/10.1080/01425692.2011.596372.

Collins-Mayo, S. and Dandelion, P. (eds), (2010) *Religion and youth*, Farnham, Burlington: Ashgate.

Cover, R. O. B. (2016) *Queer youth suicide, culture and identity: Unliveable lives?* London: Routledge.

Denzin, N. K. (2010) *Childhood socialization* (2nd rev. edn), New Brunswick: Transaction Publishers.

Duranti, A., Ochs, E. and Schieffelin, B. B. (eds), (2014) *The handbook of language socialization. Blackwell Handbooks in Linguistics*, Malden: Wiley Blackwell.

Durkheim E. (1956/1902). *Education and sociology*, New York: Free Press.

Easterby-Smith, M. and Lyles, M. A. (eds) (2011) *The Blackwell handbook of organizational learning and knowledge management*, Chichester: Wiley.

Erikson, E. H. (1968) *Identity: Youth and crisis*, New York: Norton.

Erikson, E. H. (1964) *Insight and responsibility: Lectures on the ethical implications of psychoanalytic insight*, New York: Norton.

Flanagan, C. (1999) *Early socialisation: Sociability and attachment*, London: Routledge.

Fong, R. (ed) (2004) *Culturally competent practice with immigrant and refugee children and families*, New York: Guilford Press.

Freud, S. (1927). *The ego and the ID* (J. Riviere, Trans.), London: Hogarth Press (Original work published 1923).

Grusec, J. E. and Hastings, P. D. (eds) (2016) *Handbook of socialization: Theory and research* (2nd edn), New York: The Guilford Press.

Habermas, J. (1984) *The theory of communicative action: Reason and the rationalization of society* (1st vol.) (T. A. McCarthy, Trans.), Boston: Beacon (Original work published 1981).

Habermas, J. (1987) *The theory of communicative action: Life world and system: A critique of functionalist reason* (2nd vol.) (T. A. McCarthy, Trans.), Boston: Beacon (Original work published 1981).

Havighurst, R. J. (1953) *Developmental tasks and education*, New York: Longman.

Hurrelmann, K. (1988) *Social structure and personality development: The individual as a productive processor of reality*, New York: Cambridge University Press.

Hurrelmann, K. (1989) *Human development and health*, Berlin, Heidelberg: Springer.

Hurrelmann, K. and Quenzel, G. (2013) *Lebensphase Jugend: Eine einführung in die sozialwissenschaftliche Jugendforschung* (12. korrigierte Auflage) [Adolescence as a phase of life: An introduction to sociological youth research (12th rev. edn)], Weinheim, Basel: Beltz Juventa.

Hurrelmann, K. and Ulich, D. (eds) (1980) *Handbuch der Sozialisations forschung* (1. Auflage) [Handbook of socialization research (1st edn)], Weinheim, Basel: Beltz.

ISSC, IDS and UNESCO. (2016) *World social science report 2016: Challenging inequalities: Pathways to a just world*, Paris: UNESCO Publishing.

Killen, M. and Smetana, J. G. (eds) (2007) *Handbook of moral development*, New York: Taylor & Francis.

Kirby, J. B. and Kaneda, T. (2006) 'Access to health care: does neighborhood residential instability matter?', *Journal of Health and Social Behavior*, *47*(2): 142–155. doi:10.1177/00221465060470 0204.

Krijnen, T. and van Bauwel, S. (2015) *Gender and media: Representing, producing, consuming*, London, New York: Routledge.

Lancy, D. F., Bock, J. C. and Gaskins, S. (eds) (2010) *The anthropology of learning in childhood*, Walnut Creek: AltaMira Press.

Lareau, A. (2011) *Unequal childhoods: Class, race, and family life* (2nd edn), Berkeley: University of California Press.

Lehmann, W. (2005) 'Choosing to labour: structure and agency in school-work transitions', *The Canadian Journal of Sociology, 30*(3): 325–350. Retrieved from https://journals.library.ualberta.ca/cjs/index.php/CJS/index.

Lemish, D. (ed), (2013) *The Routledge international handbook of children, adolescents and media*, London: Routledge, Taylor & Francis Group.

Lerner, R. M. (1976) *Concepts and theories of human development*, Reading: Addison-Weley.

Luhmann, N. (1995) *Social systems* (J. Bednarz Jr. and D. Baecker, Trans.), Stanford: Stanford University Press (Original work published 1984).

Macmillan, R. (2001) 'Violence and the life course: the consequences of victimization for personal and social development', *Annual Review of Sociology*, *27*(1): 1–22.

Matud, M. P. (2017) 'Gender and health', in A. Alvinius (ed), *Gender differences in different contexts*, pp. 57–76. InTech, http://intecho pen.com/books/gender-differences-in-different-contexts/gender-and-health.

Mcnamee, S. (2016) *Social study of childhood*, London: Palgrave Macmillan.

Mead, G. H. (1934) *Mind, self, and society*, London: University of Chicago Press.

Parsons, T. (1951) *The social system*, New York: The Free Press.

Percy-Smith, B. and Thomas, N. (eds) (2009) *A handbook of children and young people's participation: Perspectives from theory and practice*, New York: Routledge.

Petersen, A. C., Koller, S. H., Motti-Stefanidi, F. and Verma, S. (eds) (2017) *Positive youth development in global contexts of social and economic change*, New York: Routledge.

Priest, N., Paradies, Y., Trenerry, B., Truong, M., Karlsen, S. and Kelly, Y. (2013) 'A systematic review of studies examining the relationship between reported racism and health and wellbeing for children and young people', *Social Science & Medicine*, *95*: 115–127. https://doi.org/10.1016/j.socscimed.2012.11.

Quintana, S. M. and McKown, C. (eds) (2008) *Handbook of race, racism, and the developing child*, Hoboken: Wiley.

Qvortrup, J., Corsaro, W. A. and Honig, M.-S. (eds) (2009) *The Palgrave handbook of childhood studies*, New York: Palgrave Macmillan.

Schneider, B. H. (2016) *Childhood friendships and peer relations: Friends and enemies* (2nd edn), London: Routledge.

Shell Deutschland (2015) *Jugend 2015: Eine pragmatische Generation im Aufbruch* [Youth 2015: A pragmatic generation in transition], Frankfurt: Fischer.

Simmel, G. (1890) *Über sociale Differenzierung: Sociologische und psychologische Untersuchungen* [On social differentiation: Sociological and psychological investigations], Leipzig: Duncker & Humblot.

Skelton, C., Francis, B. and Smulyan, L. (eds) (2013) *The Sage handbook of gender and education,* Thousand Oaks, Boston: Sage Publications.

Wanberg, C. R. (ed) (2012) *The Oxford handbook of organizational socialization,* New York: Oxford University Press.

Watson, J. B. (1980) *Psychology from the standpoint of a behaviorist,* London: Routledge.

Wozniak, R. H. and Fischer, K. W. (eds) (2014) *Development in context: Acting and thinking in specific environments,* New York: Psychology Press.

Index